Tips & Techniques in **English** *for Competitive Exams*

SSC/ Banking/ Insurance / Railways/ CDS/ NDA/ Hotel Mgmt./ B.Ed/ GATE

- **Corporate Office :** 45, 2nd Floor, Maharishi Dayanand Marg, Corner Market, Malviya Nagar, New Delhi-110017
  Tel. : 011-49842349 / 49842350

Access Code : Scratch the label gently

INSTRUCTIONS
1. Go to www.educoreonline.com/register.htm
2. Enter your details along with your 16 digit Access Code.
3. Click Register and you would be successfully redirected to the Login Page.
   Note: If you are already registered with us, you just have to login **(http://www.educoreonline.com/login.htm)** and enter your new 16 Character Unique Code under your Account Section.
4. Login with your registered email ID and password.
5. You can now view you free e-books under your Library.
6. You can read your e-books either Online or Offline. To read the e-books offline, simply download our Educore App and download the e-books inside the app. Educore App is available for Windows Desktop, iOS and Android.
   Note: You need to be connected to the Internet to run the interactive tests.
7. You are also welcome to visit our store **www.educoreonline.com** for your future purchases.
8. Contact us at **support@educoreonline.com** for any further assistance.

DISHA PUBLICATION
ALL RIGHTS RESERVED
Printed at Repro Knowledgecast Limited, Thane

© Copyright Publisher

No part of this publication may be reproduced in any form without prior permission of the publisher. The author and the publisher do not take any legal responsibility for any errors or misrepresentations that might have crept in. We have tried and made our best efforts to provide accurate up-to-date information in this book.

For further information about books from DISHA,
Log on to www.dishapublication.com or email to info@dishapublication.com

PREFACE

About the Book…..

Having command of English grammar isn't impossible. With a few essential grammar tips and techniques, you can overcome many of the obstacles that the aspirants of various competitive exams face. **Disha's 'Tips & Techniques in English for Competitive Exams'** contains all those tools that help you improve your English in various competitive exams.

Disha's 'Tips & Techniques in English for Competitive Exams' covers the entire syllabus for gaining clear concepts in English that consists of Fundamental Grammar including Tenses, Modals, Parts of Speech, Voices, Narrations, Phrasal Verbs, Question Tags, Transformation of Sentences, Clause Analysis, Idioms & Phrases, Spelling Rules and Contractions, etc., Vocabulary, Reading Comprehension, Parajumbles, Cloze Test, Spotting Errors, Sentence Completion, Passage Completion and many more.

'**Tips & Techniques in English for Competitive Exams**' by **Disha** is a must-have book for thorough preparation in SSC, Banking, Insurance, Railways, CDS, Hotel Management, B.Ed., Gate and various other competitive exams.

The book '**Tips & Techniques in English for Competitive Exams**' by **Disha** has been designed to explore most of the tips and techniques required for understanding English grammar and avoiding common mistakes with an ample number of examples of **Common Errors in English** and their detailed explanation .

As the book provides the information taken from sources believed to be valid and most reliable, it can prove a comprehensive guide to learning English Grammar and Composition.

Disha Experts

Index

FUNDAMENTAL GRAMMAR	**1-75**
○ Tenses	1
○ Modals	8
○ Infinitives, Gerunds and Participles	10
○ Parts of Speech	21
○ Articles	24
○ Voices	26
○ Narration	30
○ Kinds of Sentences & Clauses	35
○ Phrasal Verbs	38
○ Question Tags	41
○ Idioms and Phrases	43
○ Sentence Structure	48
○ Punctuation	58
○ Contraction	63
○ Common Errors	67
VOCABULARY	**76-103**
READING COMPREHENSION	**104-112**
○ Objective Comprehension	104
PARAJUMBLES	**113-119**
○ Rearranging Words or Sentences	113
CLOZE TEST	**120-124**
○ Filling in Paragraph Gaps or Numbered Gaps	120
SPOTTING ERRORS	**125-131**
SENTENCE COMPLETION	**132-137**
PASSAGE COMPLETION	**138-140**
REVISION EXERCISES	**141-184**

E-book 1: Practice Exercises with Hints and Solutions
E-book 2: 10 Practice Sets
E-book 3: Past Solved Papers

FUNDAMENTAL GRAMMAR

Chapter 1: TENSES

Tense is the form taken by a verb to indicate time and continuance or completeness of an action or event.
Tenses are of three main types viz. Present Tense, Past Tense and Future Tense. Further, each of these is sub-divided into four categories i.e. Simple Tense, Continuous Tense, Perfect Tense and Perfect Continuous Tense.

(I) PRESENT TENSE

It expresses an action that is currently going on or habitually performed, or a state that currently or generally exists.
Examples: She *plays* hockey and then *goes* home.
  He *goes* to dance classes.
  I *get up* every day at four o'clock in the morning.
  Sun *rises* in the east.

(1) Simple Present Tense – It is used to describe universal truths, habits, unchanging situations and scheduled activities.
Examples for repeated or regular actions in the present time period:
  ➢ I *take* the tram to the office.
  ➢ Prakash *works* eight hours every day.
  ➢ The train to Mumbai *leaves* at 10 P.M.

Examples for facts:
  ➢ We *belong* to India.
  ➢ Sun *sets* in the west.
  ➢ The president of the USA *lives* in the White House.

Examples for habits:
  ➢ They *travel* to their farmhouse every weekend.
  ➢ She *brushes* her teeth twice a day.
  ➢ I *get* up early every day.

Formation of Simple Present Tense:
  ➢ The first person (I) takes the first form of verb like- I *go* and I *work* there etc.
  ➢ The second person (You) takes the first form of verb like- You *come* and You *run* etc.
  ➢ In the third person singular number, the verb always ends with 's' like- He *wants*, She *gives*, She *thinks* and She *runs* etc. In case the verb is ending with 'y', it changes to 'ies' like- She *flies* and He *cries* etc.
  ➢ In the third person plural number, the first form of verb is used like- They *come* and They *go* etc.

(2) Present Continuous Tense – It is used for those actions which are happening now or are unfinished. This tense is also used when the action is temporary and it is also known as Present Progressive Tense.

Examples:
- He is *weeping*.
- She is *talking* with the guests.
- The baby is *sleeping* in the crib.

Present Continuous Tense is also used to express something not happening right now or will not happen in the near future, for example- You are not *watching* the game, She is not *sitting* over there and I am not *going* to the meeting after work etc. Moreover, The Present Continuous Tense is also used in questions as well, for example- Is he *laughing*?, Are you *coming*? and Are they *listening* to the teacher? etc.

(3) Present Perfect Tense – It is used to indicate the completion of an activity or an action that occurred at some point in the past. Though, the time of the action is not exactly known, this tense is mostly used to refer to actions completed in the immediate past (not a very long time ago).

Examples:
- I *have eaten* my meal.
- I *have finished* cooking.
- He *has bought* a car.

Note:
In the present perfect sentences, the past participle of 3rd form of verb is used with the auxiliary verbs 'has' or 'have 'depending upon the subject of the sentence. For example, if the subject of the sentence is 'She, He, It or a singular noun' then the auxiliary verb 'has' is used and when the subject of the sentence is 'They, You or a plural noun' then the auxiliary verb 'have' is used.

Examples:
- She *has qualified* the exam.
- They *have helped* us.
- You *have done* a good job.
- He *has not started* a business.
- It *has come*.

(4) Present Perfect Continuous Tense – It is used for an action which started in the past and is continuing at the present time. A time reference is also used in the sentence to show the time of action. The specific words 'since' and 'for' are used to show the time of action.

'Since' is used if the exact starting time of action is known like - since Sunday and since 6 A.M etc. and on the other hand, 'For' is used to express the amount of time like - for 10 days and for six months etc.

TENSES

The auxiliary verbs 'have been' or 'has been' is used depending upon the subject of the sentence. If the subject of the sentence is 'She, He, It or a singular noun' then the auxiliary verb 'has been' is used and if the subject of the sentence is 'They, You or a plural noun' then the auxiliary verb 'have been' is used.

Structure: Subject + Auxiliary verb + Main verb + Time-reference and Subject + Have been/ Has been + Present Participle (verb+ing) + Time-reference

Examples:
- He *has been living* in the USA *since* 1990.
- She *has been working* in this company *since* 2002.
- He *has been studying* this book *for* three months.
- They *have been waiting* for me *for* three hours.
- Ravi *has been writing* for this newspaper *since* 25th May, 2007.
- I *have been watching* the movie *for* two hours.

Some examples of interrogative sentences are:
- Has *she been working* as a professor *for* five years?
- Have *they been making* a noise *for* two hours?
- Has *she been writing* the report *since* 1st March, 2016?
- Has *your mother been teaching* you *since* 2001?

(II) PAST TENSE

It expresses an action or event that has happened or a state that previously existed.

Examples:
- He *went* home yesterday.
- The work *was finished* on 4th June.
- She *worked* in a sugar factory.
- My father *believed* in superstitions.

(1) Simple Past Tense – It is used to talk about a completed action in a time before now. The time of the action can be in the recent past or the distant past.

Examples for an action completed in the past:
- The steamer *sailed* yesterday.
- He *went* home some time back.
- She *used to* carry an umbrella.

(2) Past Continuous Tense – It is used to mention an ongoing action of the past or an action that continued sometime in the past. It is also known as Past Progressive Tense. In these sentences, 1st form of the verb + ing and auxiliary verbs 'was' or 'were' is used depending upon the subject of the sentence. If the subject of the sentence is 'I, She, He or a singular noun then the auxiliary verb 'was' is used and if the subject of the sentence is 'You, They or a plural noun then the auxiliary verb 'were' is used.

Examples:
- He *was waiting* for his mother.
- She *was riding* a bike.
- The dog *was barking* at them.
- I *was planning* for the holidays.
- They *were eating* their meal.
- You *were not preparing* for the exam.

(3) Past Perfect Tense – It is used to show that something happened before another action in the past or simply, it is used to express two actions that happened in the past. Moreover, in this case, it is necessary to show which action/event happened earlier than the other.

Examples:
- I *had done* my homework when Hari *came* to see me.
- They *lost* many games because *they had* not practised enough.
- You *had studied* French before you *moved* to Italy.
- When I *reached* the station, the train *had departed*.
- I *had just gone* out when it *started* raining.

(4) Past Perfect Continuous Tense – It is used when an action/event that began before a certain point of time in the past and was continuing at the given point of time in the sentence. The sentence includes a 'time-reference' i.e. 'since' and 'for' to show when the action started in past or for how long the action was continued in the past.

Sentence structure:
Subject + Auxiliary verb + Main verb + Time-reference
Subject + Had been + Present Participle + Object + Time-reference

Examples:
- She *had been watching* the game *for* two hours.
- He *had been working* for a newspaper *for* seven years.
- I *had been applying* for jobs *since* May 2013.
- She *had been teaching since* October, 2010
- Had *she been waiting* for her husband *for* three years.

(III) FUTURE TENSE

It expresses an action/event that has not yet happened or a state that does not yet exist.

Examples:
- I *will* go there.
- They *will* not play football.
- I *shall* meet him if he calls me.

TENSES

(1) Simple Future Tense – It is used to express an action that will occur or happen in the future.

Examples:
- I *will* buy a laptop at the end of this month.
- We *will* shift to a new apartment the next week.
- My father *will* buy me a bicycle on my birthday.
- He *will* leave for Canada day after tomorrow.
- She *will* get admission in a new school.

(2) Future Continuous Tense – It is used to express an on-going or continued action which will occur at some time in the future. In these sentences, the first form of the verb + ing is used along with the auxiliary verbs 'will be or 'shall be'.

Examples:
- He ***will be singing*** a song for the audience.
- I ***shall be reading*** the paper then.
- He ***will be meeting*** us next week.
- I ***will be writing*** a report.

(3) Future Perfect Tense – It is used to indicate the completion of an action/event in the future. In these sentences, the third form of the verb is used with the auxiliary verbs 'will have' or 'shall have'.

Examples:
- I ***shall have written*** my exercise by that time.
- He ***will have completed*** his project by Sunday.
- I ***will have taken*** my lunch.
- He ***would have finished*** his task.

(4) Future Perfect Continuous Tense – It is used to indicate an action represented as being in progress over a period of time that will end in the future. Time period is generally mentioned along with it. 'Since' or 'for' is used in the sentence for time-reference. In these sentences, first form of the verb + ing is used along with the auxiliary verbs 'will have been' or 'shall have been'.

Examples:
- By next July, we shall have been living here for four years.
- The child will have been sleeping since 10 P.M.
- The doctor will have been treating patients for three years.
- You will have been using my bike for six months.
- The company will not have been advertising posts for two years.

TENSES

TENSES IN A NUTSHELL:

Tenses		Present	Past	Future
Simple	Rule :	Subject + V1 Form	Subject + V2 Form	Subject + will + V1 Form
	When to be used :	Universal Truths, planned and scheduled activities, description of routines.	Activity started in the past, got over in the past.	Only when there is possibility of the activity happening, not certainity.
Continuous	Rule :	Subject + is/am/are + ING Form	Subject + was/were + ING Form	Subject + Will be + ING Form
	When to be used :	When an Activity started some time ago, is still continuing while speaking.	An activity is going on. Before it is over, it is interrupted by another activity.	There is a certainity of the Activity happening in the future.
Perfect	Rule :	Subject + Has/Have + V3 Form	Subject + has + V3 Form	Subject + Will have + V3 Form
	When to be used :	When an Activity is over but it still has an effect on the present.	An activity started in the past and was concluded. Another Activity also happened. REFERS TO ACTIVITY 1.	Refers to Activity 1, which will have been completed, by the time Activity 2 happens.
Perfect Continuous	Rule :	Subect + has been + ING Form + Since/for	Subject + had been + ING Form + since/for	Subject + Will have been + ING Form + since/for
	When to be used :	An Activity started in the past but we are not sure when it will conclude/end.	NOT USED IN CONVERSATIONAL ENGLISH	NOT USED IN CONVERSATIONAL ENGLISH

TENSES

Additional notes:
- Events occurring at the same time must be given in the same tense.

Examples

When he *fainted*, his brother *was* with him; When he *was writing* his report, his mother *was preparing* meal for him, etc.

- Will or Shall can't be used twice in the same sentence even if both the actions refer to future tense.

Examples

I shall come if he will call me. **(WRONG)**
I shall come if he calls me. **(RIGHT)**

- With the phrase 'as if 'or 'as though', the past tense and plural form of the verb should be used.

Examples - He behaves *as if* he *were* the owner.
It looks *as if* they *have had* a shock.
It looks *as though you've* not *met* him before.

- With the word 'wish', four verbs are used namely, *were, had, could and would.*

'*Were*' is used when the wish seems to be unrealizable like, I wish I were a king.

'*Had*' is used when our wish is lament over the past happening like, I wish I had accepted that offer.

'*Would*' is used when we refer to the future like I wish I would get a ticket.

'*Could*' is used when we wish that something which has already happened should have happened otherwise like, He did not go because he was busy yesterday, I wish he could go with you.

Chapter 2
MODALS

Modals are verbs that are used to indicate modality i.e. the mood or the attitude of the speaker which may be likelihood, ability, obligation, request, wish, duty and suggestion etc. The commonly used modals are can, could, may, might, would, shall, should, need, must and ought etc.

MODALS	USAGE	EXAMPLES
Can	To express ability	I can speak Russian fluently.
Can	To request permission	Can I open the door?
Could	To request politely	Could you please do it for me?
May	To express possibility	It may rain.
May	To request permission	May I come in?
May	Wish or Prayer	May you live long!
May	Purpose	He works hard so that he may pass.
Might	Less possibility	She might be sleeping now.
Must	To express obligation	You must leave now.
Must	To express strong belief	He must be over 80 years old.
Must	Logical certainty	Living alone in such a big city must be difficult.
Should	To give advice	You should stop smoking.
Should	Duty/Obligation	We should obey the laws.
Should	To express probability	She should be in the temple.
Would	To request or Offer	Would you like to have a cup of tea?
Would	Habitual action or Past Routine	She would study at noon.
Would	Wish	I would be glad to help you.

MODALS

Ought * (It is stronger than both should and must.)	To express moral obligation	We ought to love our parents.
Will	Wish, Request, Demand	Will you please pick up the phone?
Will	Prediction, Assumption	I think it will rain on Monday.
Will	Promise	I will quit smoking.
Will	To express habits	Her mom is strange; she will sit for hours without talking.
Need not	To express an action which is not necessary	He need not go there again.

Chapter 3
INFINITIVES, GERUNDS AND PARTICIPLES

Infinitives, Gerunds and Participles are verb forms that perform peculiar functions, other than principal verbs in sentences. They are called verbals.

INFINITIVES

Infinitives are, basically, *to+verb* phrases functioning as nouns.
They follow verbs such as agree, begin, continue, decide, fail, hesitate, hope, intend, learn, neglect, offer, plan, prefer, pretend, promise, refuse, remember, start, try that require no agent of action; and advise, allow, convince, remind, encourage, force, hire, teach, instruct, invite, permit, tell, implore, incite, appoint, order which need an agent of action.

FORM: **To + verb**

Stemming from the **To + verb** formula, infinitives appear in various forms as under:

(i) To + V1 [present infinitive, active voice]

Examples:
- Most children hate *to study*.
- Try as you may, you are not cut out *to succeed*.
- He promised *to deliver* but his credibility was suspect.
- The employees were asked *to furnish* the details of their assets.
- This team is expected *to win* the match.

(ii) To + be + V2 [present infinitive, passive voice]

Examples:
- Young and old alike crave *to be appreciated*.
- Some great men walk the earth *to be revered* forever.
- Though extremely talented, he was destined *to be doomed*.
- Derek bolted like a bullet even as Sam appeared *to be hurt*.
- Having prepared an excellent meal, he was sure *to be lauded* by the guests.

(iii) To + have + V3 [perfect infinitive, active voice]

Examples:
- Mother seems *to have forgotten* to shut the door.
- I remember *to have met* her in your birthday party.
- He claims *to have seen* them sneak into the premises.

INFINITIVES, GERUNDS AND PARTICIPLES

- The duo is reported *to have stolen* all the valuables in the house.
- They are believed *to have spoken* the truth.

(iv) To + have been + V3   [perfect infinitive, passive voice]

Examples:

- He seemed *to have been warned* of dire consequences.
- She appeared *to have been taken* for a ride.
- The witness looked *to have been harassed* by the police.
- The sky appeared *to have been washed blue* after the downpour.
- They admitted *to have been mistaken* in viewing her negatively.

(v) To + be + V1-ing   [continuous infinitive]

Examples:

- You seem *to be enjoying* the show very much.
- The traffic seems *to be delaying* the arrival of the minister.
- He is too artless *to be lying* through his teeth.
- Terrorists are perceived *to be seeking* attention through their misdeeds.

(vi) To + have been + V1-ing   [perfect continuous infinitive]

Examples:

- The clerk confessed *to have been helping* the embezzlers.
- The fugitive was reported *to have been living* with a nomadic tribe.
- Failed and defeated, he was suspected *to have been contemplating* suicide.
- The movie looked *to have been doing well* before protesters brought it down.
- They appear *to have been going* the wrong way.

[*Note: Passive voice is not possible in continuous forms*]

(vii) [To] Verb   [bare infinitive or direct infinitive]

Bare infinitives associate with specific words as discussed below:

▶ the verbs **make, bid, see, hear, feel, know, watch, help, let, have, expect** with the <u>agent</u> of the action

Examples:

- He made <u>them</u> [to] *see* the truth behind the apparent.
- They bade <u>him</u> [to] *ascend* the stage and *speak.*
- It made <u>him</u> [to] *feel* the pain of the sufferers.
- The incident helped <u>them</u> [to] *know* their servants as human beings.
- You helped <u>me</u> [to] *overcome* my depression.
- I watched the <u>ship</u> [to] *disappear* down the horizon.
- I saw <u>them</u> [to] *leave* in a huff.
- On his request, the administration let <u>him</u> [to] *preside* over the conference.
- I will not have <u>you</u> [to] *scold* him for no fault of his.

INFINITIVES, GERUNDS AND PARTICIPLES

- **need** and **dare** only as auxiliaries in negative and interrogative forms

Examples:
- Mother, you need not [to] *worry* for me.
- Need you [to] *work* so hard?
- Dare he [to] *cross* the forest in the dark?
- I dare not [to] *question* his authority.

- **and, but, or, except, as... as, than**

Examples:
- He did nothing more **than** [to] play the whole day.
- The banished people had nothing to do **except** [to] *curse* their fate.
- He liked to travel **as** much **as** [to] *wander* in the forests.
- Would you want to finish the work **or** [to] *have* your dinner first?
- The activists do nothing **but** [to] make people aware of the anomalies.
- Isn't it foolish to fight **and** [to] complain of injuries?

- **better, rather, , sooner... than, as soon...as** in combination with **would** or **had**

Examples:
- The invitees **would better/had better** [to] *leave* as it is quite late.
- He **would rather/had rather** [to] *start* if he hopes to meet the deadline.
- She **would as soon** [to] *sing* **as** [to] *dance*.
- I **would sooner** [to] *fight and die* **than** [to] *surrender*.

{*Note*: All these phrases are synonyms of 'prefer', which itself takes a 'gerund' instead of an 'infinitive'; e.g., Soldiers prefer *dying* for the country.}

SOME SPECIAL ADDITIONS WITH INFINITIVES

- **How + infinitive**

This construction is followed by **show, know, teach, learn, ask, tell, remember, forget, discover,** and **find,** etc., to express manner or method.

Examples:
- Let me show you *how to operate* this new device.
- They know *how to deal* with the situation.
- The class is learning (how) *to create* a story in dialogues.
- This should be enough to teach him *how to respect* his elders.
- We shall ask the instructor *how to go* about it.
- So far so good, now tell me *how to conclude* the dissertation.
- I am sorry; I do not remember *how to solve* this kind of problems.
- Curiously, he forgot *how to unravel* the maze he had himself created.

INFINITIVES, GERUNDS AND PARTICIPLES

- The mission discovered *how to harvest* relevant data from the junk.
- He is desperate to find out *how to impress* the girl he fancies.

▶ **Noun + infinitive**

Preposition is essential in some infinitives following a noun to complete the sense.

Examples:
- As long as you are engaged, please give me a book *to read*. (no preposition)
- Can I have a glass of water *to drink?* (no preposition)
- I am afraid, I have no pen *to write* **with**. (preposition required)
- They are looking for a penthouse *to live* **in**. (preposition required)

▶ **Adjective + infinitive**

Too is used before the adjective to convey a negative sense; **Enough** is used after the adjective to convey a positive meaning.

Examples:
- I am **too** tired *to venture* any further.
- This is **too** good *to be* true.
- She is smart **enough** *to deal* with any untoward incident.
- The foundation should be strong **enough** *to bear* the impact of any tremor.

ERRONEOUS USE OF THE SPLIT INFINITIVE

Insertion of an adverb within an infinitive is an oft-committed mistake that must be avoided.

Examples:
- I request you *to kindly grant* me the said leave. (incorrect)
- I request you *kindly to grant* me the said leave. (correct)
- The audience was instructed to *quietly take* their seats. (incorrect)
- The audience was instructed *to take* their seats *quietly*. (correct)

FUNCTION: As a *Noun* (subject of verb, object of verb, object of preposition, subjective or objective complement), *Adjective,* or *Adverb.*

As subject of verb :
- *To err* is human; *to forgive*, divine.
- *To wait and watch* is the only option we have.
- *To pass the buck* is easy.

As object of verb :
- The president-elect promised *to deliver* on the promises.
- The college staff threatened *to strike* work.
- He manages *to balance* work and home effortlessly.

As object of preposition :
- The invaders had no option but *to surrender*.
- Vagabonds love nothing except *to wander*.
- He lives a pauper only *to die* a millionaire.

As objective complement :
- Alia asked her *to leave* as it was getting dark.
- They wanted him *to lead* the team.
- No student wished the examinations *to stay*.

As subjective complement
- My parents' desire is *to see* me well settled in life.
- The mark of a true man is *to behave* courteously.
- The delegation called *to apprise* him of the situation.

As adjective
- Napoleon nurtured the ambition *to rule* the world.
- Man is driven by the desire *to make* a name for himself.
- The play is too satiric *to earn* critical acclaim.

As adverb
- We must work *to make* this happen.
- These kids are anxious *to learn*. (adverb)
- He was pained *to see* the widespread destruction. (adverb)

GERUNDS

Gerunds are the ***V1-ing*** form of verbs functioning as nouns.

FORM: V1-ing

Retaining the ***V1-ing*** form, gerunds appear in specific constructions as under:

(i) Direct gerund

Direct gerunds are often preceded by

▶ verbs such as **consider, propose, practise, risk, regret, resist, prefer, enjoy, love, like, dislike, hate, detest, start, finish, begin, stop, miss,** etc.

Examples:
- I have requested them to consider *using* the new technology.
- Will you stop *screaming* like that, please?
- It is high time they began *accepting* the change.

▶ phrases such as **can't** (or **couldn't**) **help** and **it is no use/good**

Examples:
- They couldn't help *praising* her effusively.
- She can't help *lying* through her teeth.
- It is no use *crying* over spilt milk.
- It is no good *trying* to reform this serial offender.

INFINITIVES, GERUNDS AND PARTICIPLES

▶ verbs such as **forgive, pardon, hate, like, miss** and phrasal verbs, such as **don't mind, fed up of, give up,** in combination with a noun in the possessive case(**Ravi's, my mother's, boys'**, etc.) or a possessive adjective (**my, his, her, their,** etc.)

Examples:
- Teachers hate students' *speaking* out of turn.
- Please forgive their *trespassing* for one last time.
- Nobody misses my *singing* as much as she does.
- He doesn't mind his father's *scolding* so much.
- I am fed up of his *frowning* and *scowling*.
- She seems to have given up her *masquerading*.

(ii) **preposition + gerund**

▶ Gerunds mostly appear in this very construction usually with **prepositions other than 'to'**.

- Some phrases that precede gerunds are:
- aim at, abstain from, bent on, break free from, call for, confident of, dissuade from, desirous of, end up, fond of, harm in, intent on, interested in,
- keep on, prohibit from, refrain from, sick of, take pride in, wary of, yearn for,
- zealous in

Examples:
- These aspirants are desirous of *making* a name for themselves.
- The delegation is wary of *trying* after a series of setbacks.
- There is no harm in *accepting* one's mistake.
- They seem to be intent on *proving* him wrong.
- They yearned for *having* a glimpse of the star.

▶ The preposition '**for**' + gerund is used to convey **reason/cause** or **purpose**. Use of **to** (i.e., infinitive form) in such cases is erroneous and must be avoided.

Examples:

Reason/cause :
- He is infamous for *creating* disturbance during office hours.   (**correct**)
- He is infamous to *create* disturbance during office hours.   (**incorrect**)

Purpose :
- This is for ensuring the safety of inmates.   (**correct**)
- This is to ensure the safety of the inmates.   (**incorrect**)

▶ Gerunds follow the **preposition 'to'** only when they are preceded by phrasal verbs containing **to**, such as given to, accustomed to, prone to, used to, boil down to, in addition to, with a view to, look forward to, etc.

Examples:
- We were used to *driving* through the rough countryside.
- The poor are prone to *contracting* diseases.
- The guests looked forward to *hosting* the next get-together.

FUNCTION: As a **Noun** (subject of verb, object of verb, subjective complement or object of preposition).

As subject of verb :
- *Hiking* in the hilly terrains is his favourite pastime.
- *Smoking* is injurious to health.
- *Seeing eye to eye* (gerund phrase) is a prerequisite for any association.

As object of verb :
- All the members of the council supported *voting*.
- Jaden wanted his parents to accept his *dancing*.
- She detested *my gifting her friend a watch (gerund phrase)*.

Gerund as subjective complement :
- What the locality urgently needs is *desilting of its drains (gerund phrase)*.
- Every employee knows *performing as the success mantra (gerund phrase)*.

Gerund as object of preposition:
- The law incriminates one for *impersonaing*.
- The accountant was neck deep in *embezzling*.

Distinguishing between infinitives and gerunds
- adjectives are mostly followed by infinitives rather than gerunds
- all prepositions (excluding **but** and **except**) are followed only by gerunds
- specific verbs are followed either by gerunds or, infinitives
- infinitives as well as gerunds can be subjects of verbs; only their forms distinguish them, e.g.

    To keep clean is a step closer to God.

    Keeping clean is a step closer to God.
- objects (of verbs) referring to people(nouns/pronouns) are followed only by infinitives

TIPS AND TECHNIQUES
- Identify the word preceding the verbal.
- If it is an adjective, an infinitive should follow.
- If it is a verb, recall which verbal follows that particular verb.
- If it is a simple verb with an agent of action, an infinitive should follow.
- If it is a preposition other than 'but' or 'except', a gerund should follow. In case of 'but' or 'except', a direct infinitive should follow.
- If it is a phrasal verb with 'to', a gerund should follow.
- If it is a noun/pronoun as the object of a verb, an infinitive should follow.

INFINITIVES, GERUNDS AND PARTICIPLES

In some cases, a gerund is interchangeable with an infinitive

He works for *providing* smart solutions.

He works *to provide* smart solutions.

PARTICIPLES

Participles are the present participle verb forms (*V1-ing*); past participle verb forms (*V3*); or perfect participle verb forms (*having* + *V3*); functioning as adjectives. They appear as absolute participles or participial phrases. As phrases, they include other words that modify the state or action expressed.

FORMS: (i) V1-ing   [present participle]

Absolute participles :

Examples:
- The *breaking* news about the arrest of the celebrity took everyone by surprise.
- She had known him since his *singing* days.
- All the brouhaha about their *scathing* remarks soon died down.

Phrase participles :

Examples:
- The hurricane, wreaking *havoc in the city*, struck the homeless the hardest.
- Strolling *in the lawn*, I saw a deadly cobra slipping away into the bushes.
- *The* mendicant, wandering *unaware,* was easily nabbed by the police.

(ii) V3   [past participle]

Absolute participles :

Examples:
- The *broken* window pane gave a glimpse of the penury inside.
- The need of the hour is an overhaul of the *distorted* system.
- Everyone present vouched for the *uncorrupted* innocence of the accused.

Phrase participles :

Examples:
- The minister ordered an enquiry, *in reference to the* destroyed *network*.
- *Undeterred by his* singed *hands*, he continued to rescue people from the fire.
- He revealed, he had acted on instinct, *unmindful of the* given *outcome*.

*(iii) **Having** + V3*   [perfect participle]
- Perfect participles generally appear in phrases.

INFINITIVES, GERUNDS AND PARTICIPLES

Phrase participles :

Examples:
- ***Having completed*** her work, she went out to play with her friends.
- The management acknowledged ***having released*** *the festival bonus.*
- He boasted of ***having won*** *every match he had played till date.*

FUNCTION: As ***Adjectives***

As direct adjectives :
- As direct adjectives, participles qualify nouns/pronouns and are replaceable by
adjective clauses.

Examples:
- The intruder sneaked into the house, dodging the *perambulating* watchman.
  (Here, the present participle *perambulating* qualifies the noun *watchman;* and can be replaced with the adjective clause *who was perambulating*)
- He didn't mind buying a *used* vehicle if it was in a working condition.
  (Here, the past participle *used* qualifies the noun *vehicle;* and can be replaced with the adjective clause *which had been used*)

As adverbial adjectives :
- As adverbial adjectives, participles qualify nouns/pronouns and are replaceable by
- adjective clauses or adverb clauses.

Replaceable by adjective clause

Examples:
- He came across a farm girl ***carrying*** *a bundle of hay.*
- He came across a farm girl *who was carrying a bundle of hay.*
- H***aving played*** *200 matches*, the cricketer announced retirement.
- The cricketer who had *played 200 matches* announced retirement.

Replaceable by adverb clause of time :

Example:
- ***Ferrying*** *passengers across the river*, the boatman would sing folksongs.
- *As he ferried his passengers across the river*, the boatman would sing folksongs.

Replaceable by adverb clause of condition :

Examples:
- You may ruin your chances by ***doing*** *this.*
- You may ruin your chances *if you do this.*
- But for your ***saving*** *the situation,* we had lost it.

INFINITIVES, GERUNDS AND PARTICIPLES

> *If you had not saved the situation,* we had lost it.
> *Without/not **keeping** a standby,* one is likely to be left high and dry.
> *If one doesn't keep a standby,* one is likely to be left high and dry.

Replaceable by adverb clause of reason :

Example:

> ***Being*** *careless,* they were in for a rebuke.
> They were in for a rebuke, *as/since/for/because they were careless.*

Replaceable by adverb clause of contrast :

Examples:

> *Despite/in spite of **showing** potential,* he was not considered.
> *Even though/although/though he showed potential,* he was not considered.
> *For all/ notwithstanding its smart **showcasing**,* the proposal was rejected.
> *Even though/although/though it was showcased smartly,* the proposal was rejected.

Participles are also replaceable by coordinate clauses :

Examples:

> Everyone gathered there ***laughing*** *merrily.*
> Everyone gathered there and they *were laughing merrily.*

ERRONEOUS USE OF A DANGLING OR MISRELATED PARTICIPLE :

Participles must connect to their subjects. If a particle is without a subject (dangling), or attached to the wrong subject (misrelated participle), it distorts the meaning of the sentence.

Examples:

> *Being* a bright sunny day, we had a game of cricket.   **(incorrect)**
> The participle *being* is dangling or is misrelated to 'we', the wrong subject.
> Its subject is 'a bright sunny day'; so, the pronoun 'it' should be used.
> **It** being a bright sunny day, we had a game of cricket.   **(correct)**
> *Taking* a stroll in the garden, a snake bit him.   **(incorrect)**

The participle *taking* is attached to 'a snake', the wrong subject.
Its subject is 'he'.

> *Taking* a stroll in the garden, **he** was bitten by a snake.   **(correct)**
> *Bullying* everyone, Rajiv's classmates avoided him.   **(incorrect)**
> The participle *bullying* is attached to 'Rajiv's classmates', the wrong subject.
> Its subject is Rajiv; so, the pronoun 'his' should be used.
> *Bullying* everyone, Rajiv was avoided by his classmates.   **(correct)**

DISTINGUISHING BETWEEN PARTICIPLES AND GERUNDS

Both, participles and gerunds, have V1-ing form. They are distinguished by their function.

Gerunds function as nouns, participles, as adjectives.

Examples:

- ➤ *Organising* is a difficult task. (Gerund)
- ➤ He was an *organising* genius. (Participle)
- ➤ He refrains from *sleeping* late into the day. *(Gerund)*
- ➤ She found her dog *sleeping* under the tree. *(Participle)*
- ➤ They were pulled up for *creating* trouble. *(Gerund)*
- ➤ Children love any kind of *creating* game. *(Participle)*

TIPS AND TECHNIQUES

- ➤ Identify whether the –ing verb is finite or non-finite (a verbal).
- ➤ If it is not preceded by any form of the auxiliary 'be' (is/am/are/was/ were/ has been/have been/ had been), it is a verbal.
- ➤ Check the position of the verbal to identify its function.
- ➤ If it precedes a verb, it is the subject of the verb or a noun; therefore, a gerund.
- ➤ If it follows a verb, it is the object of the verb or a noun; therefore, a gerund.
- ➤ If it follows a preposition, it is a noun; therefore, a gerund.
- ➤ If it precedes or follows an article, it is an adjective; therefore, a participle.
- ➤ If it precedes or follows a noun/pronoun, it is an adjective; therefore, a participle.
- ➤ If it is part of an adverbial which can be replaced with a clause, it is a participle.

Chapter 4
PARTS OF SPEECH

A part of speech is a linguistic category of words which explains how a word is used in a sentence. It is also called lexical categories, grammatical categories or word classes. There are eight parts of a speech viz. ***Noun, Pronoun, Adjective, Verb, Adverb, Preposition, Conjunction and Interjection.***

Noun: A noun is a naming word .i.e. it is used to name a person, place, thing, quality or action. Examples: India, Rajeev, Tiger, Water and Sand, Happiness etc.

Usage in sentences:
- I live in ***Australia***.
- The ***sand*** is hot.
- ***Philip*** is my elder brother.
- ***Gold*** is a precious metal.
- It makes me ***sad*** to see you looking so ***unhappy***.

Pronoun: It is a word used in place of a noun or noun phrase to avoid repetition.
Example – I, You, We, She, It, They, Those and Either etc.

Usage in sentences:
- ***I*** am taller than ***he*** is.
- ***This*** is my notebook.
- ***Whom*** did you meet?
- The watch ***that*** I bought is very costly.
- ***Either*** of the two brothers is staying here.

Adjective: It is a word naming an attribute of a noun or adds to the meaning of a noun.
Example – Sweet, Red, Heavy, Tall and Beautiful etc.

Usage in sentences:
- The box is too ***heavy*** to lift.
- This house is ***bigger*** than that one.
- She is the ***smartest*** in the class.
- She has ***five*** children.
- ***Skinny*** cats are not necessarily healthy.

Verb: It is a word or phrase that describes an action, condition or experience.
Example – Run, Teach, Feel, Keep and Come etc.

Usage in sentence:
- He *teaches* in our college.
- Austin and Monika *ride* the bus to school every morning.
- He *believes* in fairies and unicorns.
- She is *writing* her exams.
- We saw the man with long hair *waiting* for the train.

Adverb: It is a word or a phrase that modifies the meaning of an adjective, verb, or other adverb expressing manner, place, time, or degree. It is also used to modify whole sentence. Example – Slowly, Wilfully, Lightly, Very, Randomly and Truthfully etc.

Usage in sentence:
- He is *very* intelligent.
- The old lady was walking *slowly*.
- He returned *immediately*.
- She did the work *wholeheartedly*.
- She *completely* rejected his proposal.
- I *sort of* felt betrayed by you.

Preposition: It is a word or a group of words that is placed before a noun or a pronoun to indicate, place, direction and method etc. Examples – In, On, Above, Over, Under, To and Across etc.

Usage in sentence:
- The glass is *on* the table.
- The dog jumped *over* the wall.
- He is standing *beside* Manisha.
- *At noon*, I went to my dad's office to surprise him.
- *During the winter*, I always spend my time playing video games.

Conjunction: It is a word used to connect clauses or sentences or to coordinate words in the same cause. Examples – And, If, But, Or, Lest and That etc.

Usage in sentence:
- You must work *or* starve.
- My elder brother *and* my cousin have gone for hunting.

PARTS OF SPEECH

- He was annoyed *that* he was contradicted.
- I will call you *after* I arrive here.
- Many people like him *because* he is honest and hardworking.
- Go to the party *but* don't fight with anyone.

Interjection: It is the word used to express emotions. An interjection is generally punctuated with an exclamation mark. Example – Oh, Alas, Wait, Ah ha, Gosh and Hurray, etc.

Usage in sentence:

- *Wow!* That was impressive.
- *Oh, really?* I don't agree.
- *Wait!* Don't throw the pen out of the window.
- *Nice!* You got the highest marks in the exam.
- *Oh god!* He again failed in the test.

Chapter 5
ARTICLES

Articles are words used before only nouns to define their (nouns) uses in the context of the sentence. It defines whether something is specific or unspecific. There are only three types of articles namely, A, An and The. 'A' and 'An' are Indefinite articles and 'The' is a Definite article. The choice to use A and An is determined primarily by sound.

- ➤ 'A' is used before a word beginning with a consonant and a vowel giving the sound of a consonant. Example – A boy, A child, A book, A university student, A uniform and A one eyed man etc.
- ➤ 'An' is used before a word beginning with a vowel, with a mute 'h' and a consonant pronounced with the sound of a vowel. Example – An ant, An apple, An hour, An honest man, An M.L.A, An X-ray machine and An L.L.B. student.
- ➤ 'A'/'An' is used before a singular/countable common noun when it is mentioned for the first time representing no particular person or thing. Example – He needs *a book*, Twelve inches make *a foot*, *A beggar* is standing outside the gate, Please, give me *a pen,* etc.
- ➤ 'A'/'An' is used before a singular countable noun which is used to single out some person/something as a representative of a class of thing, animals and persons. Example – *A cow* is a useful animal. *A son* should be obedient, etc.
- ➤ 'A'/'An' is used before a person who is unknown to the speaker. Example – There was *a Mr. Sharma* speaking on the topic in the seminar. *A Miss Singh* was the chief guest.
- ➤ 'A'/'An' is used before a verb used as nouns. Example – For *a talk*, For *a drive* and Have *a taste,* etc.
- ➤ 'A'/'An' is used before certain phrases like – In a hurry, Feel a shame, Take a fancy, Make a noise, etc.
- ➤ 'The' is used when we talk of a particular person or a thing which is already mentioned or known. Example – The person (who is mentioned earlier) has not come yet. Let us study the chapter carefully, etc.
- ➤ 'The' is used' before proper nouns specifically, before the names of historical buildings, planets, mountain ranges, rivers, gulfs, newspapers, hotels, trains and oceans, etc. Example – The Indian ocean, The Taj Mahal, The USA, The Sahara desert, The Moon, etc.

ARTICLES

Note:
- There is no plural of 'A' and 'An'. 'Some' or 'Any' is used in case a plural is required. Example – Some cows/ any cows' some apples/any apples, etc.
- When indefinite articles i.e. 'A' and 'An' are used before proper nouns, they become common nouns. For example – She is ***a shylock***. (A miser)
- We use 'The' before a proper noun for the sake of comparison. For example – Samudra Gupta was ***the Napoleon*** of India.

Chapter 6

VOICES

Voice is the quality of a verb that indicates whether its subject acts (active voice) or is acted upon (passive voice). Therefore, a verb is said to be an action on the part of a doer/subject. The distinction between active and passive voice applies only on transitive verb. Verbs are either active or passive in voice.

In **Active Voice**, the sentence begins with a ***subject.***

Examples:

He will go to the restroom.

He has bought a plot in Mumbai.

We are going to watch a movie.

My mother read the novel in one day.

Two ministers are signing the treaty.

No one responded to her marketing advertisement.

The professor will give you instructions during the exam.

The team will celebrate its victory tomorrow.

The Kangaroo carried her baby in her pouch.

The actor posted the video on Facebook.

In **Passive Voice**, the sentence begins with the ***object.***

Examples:

The restroom will be visited by him.

A plot has been bought by him in Mumbai.

A movie is going to be watched by us.

The novel was read by my mother in one day.

The treaty is being signed by two ministers.

Her marketing advertisement was not responded by anyone.

Instructions will be given to you by the professor during the exam.

The victory will be celebrated by the team tomorrow.

The baby was carried by the Kangaroo in her pouch.

The video was posted on Facebook by the actor.

VOICES

Important Rules:

> - The place of subject and object are interchanged in the sentence.
> - We use only the 3rd form of the verb or Past Participle as the main verb in Passive Voice.
> - When a sentence in **Simple Present Tense** is changed into passive voice then 'is', 'am' or 'are' is used.

Examples:

Active Voice	Passive Voice
She writes a letter.	A letter *is* written by her.
Does he write a letter?	*Is* a letter written by him?
They sell vegetables.	Vegetables *are* sold by them.
My friend helps me.	I *am* helped by my friend.

> - When a sentence in **Present Continuous Tense** is changed into passive voice then 'is being', 'am being' or 'are being' is used.

Examples:

Active Voice	Passive Voice
She is writing a letter.	A letter *is being* written by her.
They are eating bananas.	Bananas *are being* eaten by them.
You are disturbing me.	I *am being* disturbed by you.
My friend is helping me.	I *am being* helped by my friend.

> - When a sentence in **Present Perfect Tense** is changed into passive voice then 'has been' or 'have been' is used.

Examples:

Active Voice	Passive Voice
He has completed the work.	The work *has been* completed by her.
She has cooked the food.	The food *has been* cooked by her.
I have made some cookies.	Some cookies *have been* made by me.
Has he done the work?	*Has* the work *been* done by him?

> - When a sentence in **Simple Past Tense** is changed into passive voice then 'was' or 'were' is used.

Examples:

Active Voice	Passive Voice
She bought a car.	A car *was* bought by her.
Did she buy a car?	*Was* a car bought by her?
I helped them.	They *were* helped by me.
He decorated the walls.	The walls *were* decorated by him.

> When a sentence in **Past Continuous Tense** is changed into passive voice then '**was being**' or '**were being**' is used.

Examples:

Active Voice	Passive Voice
He was cleaning the floor.	The floor *was being* cleaned by him.
Was she wearing a shirt?	*Was* a shirt *being* worn by her?
Girls were singing songs.	Songs *were being* sung by girls.
They were eating sweets.	Sweets *were being* eaten by them.

> When a sentence in **Past Perfect Tense** is changed into passive voice then '**had been**' is used.

Examples:

Active Voice	Passive Voice
They had won the game.	The game *had been* won by them.
Had they won the game?	*Had* the game *been* won by them?
He had collected donations.	Donations *had been* collected by him.
They had not done the work.	The work *had not been* done by them.

> When a sentence in **Simple Future Tense** is changed into passive voice then '**will be**' is used.

Examples:

Active Voice	Passive Voice
She will write a poem.	A poem *will be* written by her.
You will receive the letter.	The letter *will be* received by you.
They will help the poor boy.	The poor boy *will be* helped by them.
My wife will buy crockery.	Crockery *will be* bought by my wife.

VOICES

> When a sentence in **Future Perfect Tense** is changed into passive voice then '**will have been**' is used.

Examples:

Active Voice	Passive Voice
She will have received the letter.	The letter *will have been* received by her.
She will not have received the parcel.	The parcel *will not have been* received by her.
Will he have delivered the money?	*Will* the money *have been* delivered by him?
He will have done the work.	The work *will have been* done by him.

> The sentences of the **following tenses can't be changed to Passive Voices:**
- Present Perfect Continuous Tense
- Past Perfect Continuous Tense
- Future Perfect Continuous Tense
- Future Continuous Tense
- Sentences having Intransitive verbs.

Chapter 7
NARRATION

The art of conveying the words of the speaker is called Narration. Narration is of two types viz. Direct Speech and Indirect Speech.

(1) **Direct Speech** – It is a kind of speech which is conveyed by some other person exactly in the words spoken by the speaker. In this form, the actual words of the speaker are put in inverted commas.

Examples :

The President said, "We will become a developed nation in the coming ten years." In this example, *The President* is the conveyer/reporter, *said* is the reporting verb and *"We will become a developed nation in the coming ten years."* is the reported speech.

(2) **Indirect Speech** – It is a kind of speech in which some other person reports what the speaker said in his own words without quoting the exact words i.e. the actual words of the speaker are transformed and said in a simple manner by using certain conjunctions in place of commas and making necessary changes in the verbs and the pronoun of the reported speech.

Examples :

Direct speech – Monika said, "I am suffering from fever.

Indirect speech – *Monika said that she was suffering from fever.*

Important Rules to convert a Direct Speech to Indirect Speech :

RULES OF CHANGING DIRECT INTO INDIRECT SPEECH

Changes in Tenses : The past perfect and past perfect continuous tenses do not change.

	Direct Speech	Indirect Speech
Simple Present Changes To Simple Past	"I always drink tea", he said	He said that he always drank tea.
Present Continuous Changes To Past Continuous	"I am reading a book", she said.	She said that she was reading a book.
Present Perfect Changes To Past Perfect	She said, "He has finished his work"	She said that he had finished his work.

NARRATION

Present Perfect Continuous Changes To Past Perfect Continuous	"I have been to England", he told me.	He told me that he had been to England.
Simple Past Changes To Past Perfect	"Bill arrived on Saturday", he said.	He said that Bill had arrived on Saturday.
Past Perfect Changes To Past Perfect (No Change In Tense)	"I had just come back from work," he said.	He said that he had just come back from work.
Past Continuous Changes To Past Perfect Continuous	"We were living in Hong Kong", they told us.	They told us that they had been living in Hong Kong.
Future Changes To Present Conditional	"I will be in Italy on Saturday", she said	She said that she would be in Italy on Saturday.
Future Continuous Changes To Conditional Continuous	He said, "I'll be visiting mother next Monday."	He said that he would be visiting mother next Monday.
Future Changes To Present Conditional	"I will be in Italy on Saturday", she said	She said that she would be in Italy on Saturday.
Future Continuous Changes To Conditional Continuous	He said, "I'll be visiting mother next Monday."	He said that he would be visiting mother next Monday.

Words expressing nearness in time or places are generally changed into words expressing distance.

	Direct Speech	Indirect Speech
Change of place and time	Here	There
	Today	that day
	this morning	that morning
	Yesterday	the day before
	Tomorrow	the next day
	next week	the following week
	next month	the following month

	Direct Speech	Indirect Speech
Change of place and time	Now	Then
	Ago	Before
	Thus	So
	Last Night	the night before
	This	That
	These	Those
	Hither	Thither
	Hence	Thence
	Come	Go

CHANGES IN PRONOUNS

The pronouns of the Direct Speech are changed where necessary, according to their relations with the reporter and his hearer, rather than with the original speaker.

	Direct Speech	Indirect Speech
The first person of the reported speech changes according to the subject of reporting speech.	He says, "I am in fifth class."	He says that he is in fifth class.
The second person of reported speech changes according to the object of reporting speech.	He says to them, "You have completed your job."	He tells them that they have completed their job.
The third person of the reported speech doesn't change.	She says, "She is in ninth class."	She says that she is in ninth class.

CHANGES IN MODALS

	Direct Speech	Indirect Speech
CAN changes into COULD	He said, "I can touch the ceiling".	He said that he could touch the ceiling.
MAY changes into MIGHT	He said, "I may buy a house"	He said that he might buy a house.

NARRATION

MUST changes into HAD TO	He said, "I must resign from the job"	He said that he had to resign from the job.
*These Modals Do Not Change: **Would, could, might, should, ought to.***		
Would	She said, "she would apply for a visa"	She said that she would apply for a visa.
Could	He said, "I could climb the ladder."	He said that he could climb the ladder.
Might	Tom said, "I might help him".	Tom said that he might help him.
Should	She said, "I should go to the pub."	She said that she should go to the pub.
Ought to	She said to me, "you ought to wait for her."	She said to me that I ought to wait for her.

CHANGES IN IMPERATIVE SENTENCES

Imperative sentences consist any of these four: Order, request, advice and suggestion.

Mood in Direct Speech	Reporting verb in indirect verb
Order	ordered
Request	requested / entreated
Advice	advised / urged
Never	told, advised or forbade (No need of "not" after "forbade")
Direction	directed
Suggestion	suggested to
Warning	warned
(If a person is addressed directly)	called

CHANGES IN EXCLAMATORY SENTENCES

Exclamatory sentences express emotions. Interjections such as Hurrah, wow, alas, oh, ah are used to express emotions.

Rules of conversion of Exclamatory Direct Speech into Indirect Speech
1. Exclamatory sentence changes into assertive sentence.
2. Interjections are removed.
3. Exclamation mark changes into full stop.
4. Wh- words like 'what' and 'how' are removed and before the adjective of reported speech we put 'very.'

Mood in Direct Speech	Reporting verb in indirect verb
sorrow	Exclaimed with sorrow/ grief/ exclaimed sorrowfully or cried out
happiness	exclaimed with joy/ delight/ exclaimed joyfully
surprise	exclaimed with surprise/ wonder/ astonishment
appreciation	applauded

RULES OF CONVERSION OF INTERROGATIVE DIRECT SPEECH

Changes	Direct Speech	Indirect Speech Condition
Reporting Verb	said/ said to	Asked, enquired or demanded.
Joining Clause	If sentence begins with auxiliary verb	joining clause should be if or whether.
	If sentence begins with "wh-" questions	no conjunction is used as "question-word" itself act as joining clause.
Punctuation	Question Mark	Full Stop
Helping Verbs	sentences is expressing positive feeling	do/does is removed from sentence.
	if 'No' is used in interrogative sentences	do/does is changed into did.
	Did or has/have	Had

Chapter 8
KINDS OF SENTENCES & CLAUSES

In the English language, there is considerable flexibility in sentence construction. Using various sentence patterns produces speech and writing which interests the reader. Variety in sentence construction also contributes to well-organized content.

ENGLISH SENTENCE CONSTRUCTION

(1) SIMPLE SENTENCE

A **simple sentence** has the most basic elements that make it a sentence: a subject, a verb, and a completed thought.

Example:
She bought a big cake for her brother's birthday. Rina waited for her sister. Rishi and Saumya took the bus.

(2) COMPLEX SENTENCE

A complex sentence contains one independent clause and one or more dependent clause. In a complex sentence, one idea is generally more important than the other one and the more important idea is put in the independent clause while the less important idea is put in the dependent clause.

| Independent Clause + Dependent Clause |
| Dependent Clause + , + Independent Clause |

Example:
If you are not good at English, **it is pointless to apply for content writing**. When he saw the Mother coming, **he sneaked out of the house**. Shimla which is very crowded in this month of the season **is not worth visiting**.

In all the above sentences, the independent clause is in bold.

IMPORTANT: There are three kinds of dependent clauses used in complex sentences: *adverb, adjective and noun*.

1. A **dependent adverb clause** begins with an adverbial subordinator such as *when, while, because, even though, so that, etc.*
2. A **dependent adjective clause** begins with a relative pronoun such as *who, whom, which, whose,* or a relative adverb *where, when,* and *why.*
3. A **dependent noun clause** begins with *that, a wh-question word, whether,* and *if.*

(3) COMPOUND SENTENCE

The compound sentence contains two or more independent clauses but no subordinate clauses. The two independent clauses are joined by a comma (,) followed by a conjunction (for, and, nor, but...). They may also be joined by a semicolon (;), a semicolon followed by a linking adverb (therefore, however, because, since...), or a colon (:).

Example:

I don't know where she lives, and no one knew her whereabouts. (conjunction)

Alexander the Great conquered the Achaemenid Empire of Persia; he began his Indian campaign in 326 BC. (semicolon)

Joe wanted to stay with his mother; however, his father refused to keep him in the house any more. (linking adverb)

You must have heard the news: nobody is getting bonus this year! (colon)

COMPOUND SENTENCES WITH COORDINATORS

Independent Clause +, + Coordinators + Independent Clause

The two independent clauses are joined by a comma and one of the seven coordinating conjunctions: *for, and, nor, but, or, yet,* and *so*. The following sentences illustrate their meanings.

Examples:

The Japanese have the longest life expectancy of any other people, **for** their diet is extremely healthy. (**for** expresses reason)

Many Americans, on the other hand, do not take a healthy diet, **nor** do they get enough exercise. (**nor** joins two equal negative independent clauses)

COMPOUND SENTENCES WITH LINKING ADVERBS (CONJUNCTIVE ADVERBS)

Independent Clause; + Conjunctive Adverb, + Independent Clause

The two independent clauses are joined by a **semicolon** (;), a **conjunctive adverb** and a **comma**. Conjunctive adverbs express the relationship of the second clause to the first clause.

Examples:

Technical colleges offer courses for skill development for professionals; moreover, they prepare them to get a decent job in the industry. (equal related ideas)

KINDS OF SENTENCES & CLAUSES

COMPOUND SENTENCES WITH SEMICOLON

> Independent Clause + ; + Independent Clause

The two independent clauses are joined by a **semicolon** (;). Use a semicolon only when the two independent clauses are closely related and the relationship is implied.

Examples:
> Her older sister studies medicines; her younger sister studies philosophy.
>
> The Berlin Wall's construction in 1961 surprised the world; its destruction in 1989 stunned it.

(4) COMPOUND-COMPLEX SENTENCES
> A compound-complex sentence is a combination of two or more independent clauses and one or more dependent clauses.

Examples:
> After she finished college, she wanted to work in family's business, but her parents sent her abroad for further study.
>
> When the light went out, Hina was writing the essay, and Rishi was watching TV.

Types of Sentences

There are four types of sentences:

(1) Declarative Sentences: Sentences that make statements. Examples: Rishi and Kavya are neighbours. She has one brother and one sister. We are going to cinema tonight.

(2) Interrogative Sentences: Sentences that ask questions. Examples: Where are you going? Where will you go in summer holidays? Can you show me your passport?

(3) Imperative Sentences: Sentences that give commands or make requests. Examples: Get lost! Mind your business! Go and do something.

(4) Exclamatory Sentences: Sentences that are in the form of exclamations. Examples: What a good idea! How wonderful! How pretty the kitten is!

Chapter 9
PHRASAL VERBS

A phrasal verb is an idiomatic phrase consisting of a verb and other elements, either an adverb or a preposition. Typically, their meaning is not obvious from the meaning of the individual words themselves. For example – *blow up, abide by, call off, put on, etc.*

EXAMPLES OF USAGE OF PHRASAL VERBS IN SENTENCES:

Take off (to leave the ground): The plane will *take off* at 1 P.M.

Hand out (to distribute): He volunteered at the shelter where he *handed out* blankets.

Back up (to give support or encouragement, make to make a copy of): The rest of the students *backed* her *up* when she complained about the teacher to the principal.

Don't forget to *back up* your data before you format your phone.

Get away (to escape): The thieves *got away* in a stolen car.

Hurry up (to be quick or act speedily): Hurry up, guys, we have to complete the work before midnight.

BELOW IS A LIST OF SOME VERY IMPORTANT PHRASAL VERBS WITH THEIR MEANINGS:

- Ache for (want something or someone a lot)
- Auction off (sell something in an auction)
- Back away (to move backwards in fear or dislike)
- Barge in/ into (enter a place and interrupt)
- Be onto (pursue, be aware of someone's true nature)
- Beaver away (work hard)
- Bliss out (to be extremely relaxed and happy)
- Bolster up (give support, reinforce or strengthen)
- Bone up (study hard for a reason)
- Bring forth (produce something or make something known or visible)
- Buoy up (make something feel more positive)
- Butter up (praise or flatter someone excessively)
- Chicken out (be too afraid to do something)
- Chip away at (gradually reduce something to make it less powerful and effective etc.)
- Chow down (eat)
- Clamp down on (restrict or try to stop something/ to act strictly to prevent something)
- Clock up (win, score or achieve results/ ruin or spoil something)

PHRASAL VERBS

- Conjure up (create a picture or memory in someone's mind)
- Dash off (leave somewhere quickly)
- Die down (to calm down or become less strong)
- Divvy out (divide or share)
- Dole out (give out or distribute)
- Doze off (fall asleep)
- Drag on (to last longer than expected)
- Drone on (talk boringly for a long time)
- Ease off (to reduce, become less severe or slow down)
- Ebb away (disappear gradually)
- Fend for oneself (take care of oneself without help from other people)
- Ferret about (search for something)
- Gloss over (try to minimize the importance of something)
- Gnaw at (trouble, worry or annoy someone)
- Hive off (separate part of a company or service, often by selling it)
- Iron out (to resolve by discussion, to eliminate differences)
- Jockey into (persuade or deceive someone into doing something)
- Keel over (turn upside down)
- Naff off (get lost or go away - used as imperative)
- Nag at (repeatedly criticize someone verbally)
- Nod off (to fall asleep)
- Nut out (find an answer to a problem)
- Own up (to admit or confess something)
- Peck at (eat very small amounts)
- Pootle along (travel in a leisurely way)
- Psych up (prepare someone mentally)
- Queer up (mess up or ruin)
- Sally forth (leave somewhere safe or comfortable)
- Scuzz up (spill, ruin or contaminate)
- Slimmer down (become calmer or make less noise)
- Snarl up (entangle)
- Stick up for (to defend)
- Stomp off (leave somewhere angrily)
- Trot off (leave)
- Trudge through (do something slowly, with difficulty, unwillingly or considerable effort)
- Use up (To finish a product)
- Usher in (be at mark or celebrate an important point in time)
- Vamp up (make something more exciting and attractive etc.)
- Wade into (become embroiled or involved in a situation without thinking or planning usually)
- Wear out (to become unusual, to become very tired)
- Wiggle out (avoid doing)
- Yammer on (talk continuously, especially if it is an annoying way)
- Zero in on (direct or focus attention on)

IMPORTANT TIPS AND TECHNIQUES FOR PHRASAL VERB

- Frankly stating, there is no short-cut trick to solve a question based on phrasal verb. Learning them and regular reading habits can help you get good marks in this section.

- Keep on learning phrasal verbs and once you learn a phrasal verb, try to use it often while speaking or writing so that you don't forget its usage and meaning. Do it with every phrasal verb that you learn or mug up.

- Whenever you are reading or listening in English, take a note of any interesting and new phrasal verb that you come across. This helps you remember it easier and stick in your memory for a longer time.

- Be aware that one of the special features of phrasal verbs is that some of them have many different meanings. For example, you can say **pick something up** from the floor; you can **pick up** a language or bad habits; the weather can **pick up**; you can **pick up** a bargain; a radio can **pick up** a signal; the economy can **pick up**. Sometimes the meaning is clearly related, at others more literal and metaphorical.

Chapter 10: QUESTION TAGS

A question tag is a short question at the end of a statement, mostly while speaking. Question tags are used when asking for agreement or confirmation. For example – The weather is nice outside, *isn't it?*, You are coming from the market, *aren't you?*, He didn't steal the money, *did he? and* You remembered to feed the dog, *didn't you?* etc.

They are formed with the auxiliary or modal verb from the statement and the appropriate subject. It **should be noted that usually, a positive sentence is followed by a negative question tag and vice-versa.**

Examples:

POSITIVE SENTENCES, WITH NEGATIVE QUESTION TAGS

Present simple 'be'	She's Italian, **isn't she**?
Present simple other verbs	They live in London, **don't they**?
Present continuous	We're working tomorrow, **aren't we**?
Past simple 'be'	It was cold yesterday, **wasn't it**?
Past simple other verbs	He went to the party last night, **didn't he**?
Past continuous	We were waiting at the station, **weren't we**?
Present perfect	They've been to Japan, **haven't they**?
Present perfect continuous	She's been studying a lot recently, **hasn't she**?
Past perfect	He had forgotten his wallet, **hadn't he**?
Past perfect continuous	We'd been working, **hadn't we**?
Future simple	She'll come at six, **won't she**?
Future continuous	They'll be arriving soon, **won't they**?
Future perfect	They'll have finished before nine, **won't they**?
Future perfect continuous	She'll have been cooking all day, **won't she**?
Modals	He can help, **can't he**?
Modals	John must stay, **mustn't he**?

NEGATIVE SENTENCES, WITH POSITIVE QUESTION TAGS

Present simple 'be'	We aren't late, **are we**?
Present simple other verbs	She doesn't have any children, **does she**?
Present continuous	The bus isn't coming, **is it**?
Past simple 'be'	She wasn't at home yesterday, **was she**?
Past simple other verbs	They didn't go out last Sunday, **did they**?
Past continuous	You weren't sleeping, **were you**?
Present perfect	She hasn't eaten all the cake, **has she**?
Present perfect continuous	He hasn't been running in this weather, **has he**?
Past perfect	We hadn't been to London before, **had we**?
Past perfect continuous	You hadn't been sleeping, **had you**?
Future simple	They won't be late, **will they**?
Future continuous	He'll be studying tonight, **won't he**?
Future perfect	She won't have left work before six, **will she**?
Future perfect continuous	He won't have been travelling all day, **will he**?
Modals	She can't speak Arabic, **can she**?
Modals	They mustn't come early, **must they**?

Exceptions (Some verbs/expressions have different question tags):
- ✓ Question tag after 'I am' is 'aren't I?'

Example :
   I am in charge of the department, ***aren't I?***
- ✓ Positive imperative – Stop daydreaming, ***will you/won't you?***
- ✓ Negative imperative – Don't stop singing, ***will you?***
- ✓ "Let's" – Let's go to the party, ***shall we?***

TIPS AND TECHNIQUES FOR QUESTION TAGS
- ➢ Usually if the main clause in positive, the question tag is negative and if the main clause is negative, it is positive.
- ➢ If the main clause has an auxiliary verb in it, you use the same verb in the tag question. If there is no auxiliary verb (in the present simple and past simple) use do/does/did (just like when you make a normal question).

Chapter 11: IDIOMS AND PHRASES

Idioms and Phrases are two useful elements of linguistics which are often considered similar to each other and most of the time used interchangeably. However, they are different based on their meaning and readability.

A **phrase** is a small group of words standing together as a conceptual unit, while an **idiom** (also called **idiomatic expression**) is an expression, word, or phrase that has a figurative meaning conventionally understood by native speakers. This meaning is different from the literal meaning of the idiom's individual elements. In other words, idioms don't mean exactly what the words say. They have, however, hidden meaning. So, it can be said that any idiom is a phrase but all phrases are not necessarily idioms. Example – 'Raining cats and dogs' is both idiom and phrase. 'A herd of dogs' is a phrase but not an idiom.

Examples of usage of Idioms and Phrases:

- *On the tip of my tongue* which means **you are almost able to remember something, but you can't.**

    Her name was *on the tip of my tongue*, but I couldn't remember it.

- *A piece of cake* which means *very easy.*

    The exam was *a piece of cake*; I finished it in 25 minutes.

- *Fool's paradise* which means *a state of happiness based on a person's not knowing about or denying the existence of potential trouble.*

    He was living in a *fool's paradise*, refusing to accept that he was in huge debt.

- *Do you know what* my friend said? He's an audio expert and he said that we need to improve it. I don't know, *what do you think?*

- *Bring up* which means *raise children* and *mention a topic.*

    Nowadays, it is very difficult to *bring up* children.

    The matter was *brought up* to the authorities by the gatekeeper.

IDIOMS AND PHRASES

Given below are two lists of important Idioms and Phrases with their meanings:

IDIOMS	MEANING
A hot potato	Speak of a current issue which many people are talking about and which is usually disputed
A penny for your thoughts	A way of asking what someone is thinking
Add insult to injury	To further a loss with mockery or indignity; to worsen an unfavourable situation
A dime a dozen	Something common
At the drop of hat	Without any hesitation; instantly.
Back to the drawing board	When an attempt fails and it's time to start all over.
Be glad to see the back of	Be happy when a person leaves.
Beat around the bush	Avoiding the main topic
Best thing since sliced bread	A good invention; a good idea or plan.
Blessing in disguise	Something good that isn't recognized at first.
Break a leg	Good luck
Caught between two stools	When someone finds it difficult to choose between two alternatives.
Cross that bridge when you come to it	Deal with a problem if and when it becomes necessary, not before.
Curiosity killed the cat	Being inquisitive can lead you into an unpleasant situation.
Cut corners	When something is done badly to save money.
Cut the mustard	To succeed; to come up to expectations; adequate enough to compete or participate.
Cut somebody some slack	Don't be so critical.
Devil's advocate	To present a counter argument.
Don't give up the day job	You are not very good at something; You could definitely not do it professionally.

IDIOMS AND PHRASES

Elvis has left the building	The show has come to an end; it's all over.
Far cry from	Very different from
Feel a bit under the weather	Feeling slightly ill.
Get your act together	Work better or leave
Hear it on the grapevine	To hear rumours about something or someone.
Hit the nail on the head	Do or say something exactly right.
Hit the sack/sheets/hay	To go to bed.
It takes two to tango	Actions or communications need more than one person.
Jump on the bandwagon	Join a popular trend or activity.
Last straw	The final problem in a series of problems.
Method to my madness	An assertion that, despite one's approach seeming random, there actually is structure to it.
Off one's rocker	Crazy, demented, out of one's mind, in a confused or befuddled state of mind, senile.
On the wall	When someone understands the situation well.
Picture paints a thousand words	A visual presentation is far more descriptive than words.
Put wool over other people's eyes	To deceive someone into thinking well of them.
See eye to eye	To say that two or more people agree on something.
Sit on the fence	When someone does not want to choose or make a decision.
Speak of the devil	When the person you have just been talking about arrives.
Steal someone's thunder	To take credit for something someone else did.
Take with a grain of salt	This means not to take what someone says too seriously.
Whole nine yards	Everything
Wouldn't be caught dead	Would never like to do something
Your guess is as good as mine	To have no idea, do not know the answer to a question.

IDIOMS AND PHRASES

PHRASES	MEANING
Add up	Add up in number or quantity, To make sense, seem reasonable
Beef up	To make changes or an improvement.
Black out	To faint, lose consciousness
Blow up	Explode
Boil down to	To be summarized as
Break in on	Interrupt (a conversation)
Catch on	Become popular
Chicken out	To refrain from doing something because of fear.
Come about	When something happens or occurs
Come over	To visit
Do over	Repeat a job; To do something again in order to improve or correct mistakes.
Doze off	To go to sleep unintentionally
Drop by	Visit without appointment
Fall behind	To move slower than others
Flip out	To become very mad or lose control over your emotions.
Get along with	Have a good relationship with; To have good interactions with others.
Get by	survive; To pass someone or something
Goof around	To waste time doing silly or unimportant things.
Gross out	To be disgusted with someone or something.
Hit on	To suddenly have a solution to a problem or an interesting idea.
Look over	Examine, check
Look up to	Respect; To admire
Monkey around with	To try to play with or repair a device that you have no true knowledge about.
Narrow down	To reduce the number of options or possibilities.

IDIOMS AND PHRASES

Nod off	To fall asleep
Pet up to	To encourage or persuade someone to do something.
Put past	Not to be surprised by a person's actions. (Always negatively)
Put up with	Tolerate
Sneak in/into	To enter a place quietly to avoid being seen or heard.
Stick up for	To defend
Walk out on	Abandon
Watch out	To be aware of someone or something.
Wrap up	To cover something or end something

IMPORTANT TIPS AND TECHNIQUES FOR IDIOMS AND PHRASES

➤ There is no short-cut trick to solve a question based on idioms and phrases. Learning them and regular reading habits are the only options that will help you get good marks in this section.

➤ Keep learning idioms and phrases and try to use them often while speaking or writing so that you don't forget their usage and meaning. Do it with every idiom/phrase that you learn or mug up.

➤ Whenever you are reading or listening in English and come across any interesting and new idiom/phrase, make a note of it. This helps you remember them easily and stick in your memory.

Chapter 12
SENTENCE STRUCTURE

Sentences are the basic building blocks of our language. We use them to converse. And correct conversation means correct sentence usage. Thus, we need to understand different sentence structure so as to avoid grammatical errors and converse and write better. Understanding the sentence structures is essential as a lot of rules are based on them. Competitive exams always include questions on common errors/ spotting errors in sentences.

There are 4 sentence structures. But before we proceed, let us recall what clauses are. A clause is a group of words that contains at least a subject and a verb. A clause may form part of a sentence or it may be a complete sentence in itself. For example -

I have a pen made of plastic.

Here "I" is the subject and "have" is the verb.

There are two types of clauses: Independent clause and Dependent clause. For example:

When I was in Agra, I visited many famous tourist places.

The part before the comma is incomplete without the second part. If we pick only this part i.e. "When I was in Agra" it does not tell what happened when the author was in Agra. Thus it is DEPENDENT on the next part and hence is called Dependent Clause

Now look at the second part. It makes complete sense without the first one. Thus it is INDEPENDENT in existence of the previous part. This means without the previous part, it is a complete sentence in itself. Thus, it is called Independent Clause.

> **IMPORTANT:** In order to be a complete sentence, a group of words should contain a subject and a verb, and should state a complete thought. Now, let us understand the 4 sentence structures.

1. Simple Sentence: A simple sentence has one independent clause that has a subject and a verb and states a complete thought.

I won a race.

She gifted me a watch.

Deepavali is celebrated across India.

2. Compound Sentence: A compound sentence contains at least two independent clauses joined by a coordinating conjunction or a semicolon. A coordinating conjunction joins entities of equal ranks such as words, phrases, or clauses. [Most used coordinating conjunctions are F = for, A = and, N = nor, B = but, O = or, Y = yet, S = so]

SENTENCE STRUCTURE

It was raining outside, yet the children wanted to play outside.

She likes to go to parties, **but** he likes to attend conferences.

Ramesh is a good boy, **but** his brother is extremely cunning.

3. **Complex Sentence:** A complex sentence contains an independent clause and a dependent clause or a phrase joined by subordinating conjunctions. A complex sentence establishes a relation such as cause and effect, sequence, or outcome relation between the independent clause and the dependent clause.

She is studying **because she has an exam tomorrow.** [The clause in boldface is dependent clause as it shows the reason for the first clause]

While I was playing the piano, my wife was reading a book.[The clause in boldface is dependent clause as it shows the reason for the first clause]

4. **Compound-Complex Sentence:** A Compound-complex sentence contains at least two independent clauses and at least one subordinate clause. The independent clause is joined by coordinating conjunction to a complex sentence [combination of independent and dependent clause]

I was watching my favourite show, **but when I heard my mother coming, I quickly switched it off.**

[Notice that the boldface part is a complex sentence and is joined to an independent clause]

The principal wanted to scold the students, **but the teacher did not, after they apologized sincerely.** [Notice that the boldface part is a complex sentence and is joined to an independent clause]

TRANSFORMATION OF SENTENCES

Sentences can be classified into affirmative, negative, imperative, interrogative, assertive (declarative) and exclamatory sentences. They can be transformed into different forms without changing the meaning of the sentence. This process is known as transformation of sentences.

1. Affirmative Sentence

Affirmative sentence means the sentences which are used to describe any general action, event, speech, or expression.

Examples:

All students have done their homework today.

The train is always on time.

2. Assertive or Declarative Sentence

A sentence that makes a statement or assertion is called an assertive or declarative sentence. Assertive sentence ends with a period.

Examples:

She goes to market. The baby likes to play with toys. They are singing a song.

3. Interrogative Sentence

A sentence that asks a question is called an interrogative sentence. Interrogative sentence ends with question mark.

Examples:

What are you doing? Do you use your car everyday?

4. Imperative Sentence

A sentence that expresses a request, command or advice is called an imperative sentence.

Examples:

Turn off the light. (an order); Please do me a favour. (a request).

5. Exclamatory Sentence

A sentence that expresses strong feelings or emotions is called an exclamatory sentence. These sentences express surprise, joy, sorrow, appreciation, love excitement, frustration, anger etc. An exclamatory sentence ends with exclamation mark.

Examples :

What a beautiful picture it is! How nicely she is dancing! That is wonderful!

Hurrah! We have won the debate!

Transformation Rules - Affirmative to Negative Sentence

S.No.	Affirmative Sentence structure	Negative Sentence structure	Tips	Example
1.	Subject +always + verb + ext. OR Subject + auxiliary verb + always + verb/ adjective/ adverb + ext.	Subject + never opposite verb + ext. OR Subject + auxiliary verb + never + opposite verb/ adjective/ adverb + ext.	If there is always in an affirmative sentence, never will be used for ever/always in negative sentence and verb /adjective/adverb will be opposite meaning.	Affirmative: He is always on time. Negative:- He was never bothered about such incidents.

SENTENCE STRUCTURE

2.	Subject + verb + too + adjective + to + verb + ext.	Subject + verb + so + adjective + that + subject + can/ could + not + verb + ext.	If there is present tense before too, 'can' will be used after that and if there is past tense before too, 'could' will be used after that. Again when there is for + noun/ pronoun after too+ adjective, the noun/ pronoun after for will be the subject after that.	Affirmative:-He is too weak to walk. Negative:- He is so weak that he cannot walk.
3.	Subject + verb + as + adjective + as + noun/ pronoun.	Subject + auxiliary verb + not + verb + less + adjective + than + noun/ pronoun.	In negative sentence as -as is replaced by not less-than.	Affirmative: She is as tall as her sister. Negative: She is not less tall than her sister.
4.	Subject + auxiliary verb + verb/ adjective/ adverb + ext.	Subject + auxiliary verb + not + opposite verb / adjective / adverb + ext.	To change an affirmative sentence having an auxiliary verb with a verb/ adjective/ adverb into a negative sentence, add not after the auxiliary verb and use the opposite meaning of verb/ adjective/ adverb in negative sentence.	Affirmative:- I shall remember those lovely days. Negative:-I shall not forget those lovely days.
5.	Subject + verb + ext.	Subject + auxiliary verb to do + not + opposite verb + ext.	If no auxiliary verb in an affirmative sentence, to do verb will be used as auxiliary verb to make it a negative sentence. After to do verb not will be added along with the opposite verb. This to do verb will be according to the tense of the verb of affirmative sentence.	Affirmative:-He remembered her. Negative:-He did not forget her.
6.	Subject + must + verb + ext.	Subject + cannot but + verb + ext. Subject + cannot help + verb-ing + ext	To change a negative sentence into an affirmative sentence having must, use cannot but/cannot help for must. In this case, basic form of verb will be used after cannot but and present participle (verb-ing) will be used after cannot help.	Affirmative:- We must assist them financially. Negative:-We cannot but assist them financially. We cannot help assisting them financially.

#				
7.	Every + noun/ body/ one + verb + ext.	There is no + noun/ body/ one + but + verb + ext	To change an affirmative sentence having every + noun/ body/ one into a negative sentence, we can use there is no for every, then we have to put the word after every and next we should use but before verb+ ext.	Affirmative: Everybody hates a bigmouth. Negative:- There is no one but hates a bigmouth.
8.	As soon as + subject + verb (past), subject + verb(past) + ext.	No sooner had + subject + verb(past participle) + than + subject + verb(past) + ext.	To change an affirmative sentence having as soon as with two clauses, no **sooner had** will be used for as soon as in negative sentence. Than must be used between the two clauses.	Affirmative:- As soon as he reached the station, the train started. Negative:- No sooner had he reached the station than the rain started.
9.	Only + subject + verb + ext.	None but + subject + verb + ext.	Here **only** is used before a person, but **alone** is used after the person word and auxiliary verb. To change an affirmative sentence into a negative sentence where **only** is before a person or **alone** is after the person and auxiliary verb, we have to start the negative sentence with **none but** for **only/ alone.**	Affirmative:- Only God can help us. Negative:- None but God can help us.
10.	Subject + auxiliary verb + alone + ext.	None but + subject + auxiliary verb + ext.	When the subjective word is a person word i.e he/ she/ I/ you/ they/ we/ any proper noun.	Affirmative:- He was alone arrested in the case. Negative:- None but he was arrested in the case.
11.	Only + subject + verb + ext. OR Subject + verb + only + object + ext.	Nothing but + subject + verb + ext. OR Subject + verb + nothing but + object + ext.	When **only** is used before an object/thing, **nothing but** will be put to make a negative sentence from an affirmative sentence. Nothing but is used in negative sentence for only when there is an object/thing after only in affirmative sentence.	Affirmative:- Only the US has the power to veto the verdict. Negative:- None but the US has the power to veto the verdict.

SENTENCE STRUCTURE

| 12. | Subject + verb + only + number/ age + ext. | Subject + verb + not more / less than + number/age + ext. | When **only** is used before number/ age, **not more / less** than will be used in negative sentence for only in affirmative sentence. | Affirmative:- I am only 25 year old.
Negative:- I am not more/less than 25 years old. |

Transformation Rules - Assertive to Interrogative Sentence

S.no	Assertive Sentence structure	Interrogative Sentence structure	Tips	Example
1	Subject + auxiliary verb + ext.	auxiliary verb + n't + subject + ext.?	When an auxiliary verb in the assertive sentence, **n't** added and placed before the subject in the interrogative sentence	**Assertive:-** We shall go to the picnic. **Interrogative:-**Shan't we go to the picnic?
2	Subject + auxiliary verb + not + ext.	auxiliary verb + subject + ext?	When the assertive sentence is a negative sentence, the negative word will be deleted in interrogative sentence and then it will be started with only auxiliary verb.	**Assertive:-** We can not concentrate on the subject. **Interrogative:-**Can't we concentrate on the subject?
3	Subject + verb + ext.	to do + n't + subject + verb + ext?	When there is no auxiliary verb in the assertive sentence/ affirmative sentence, to change it into interrogative sentence to do verb will be used as an auxiliary verb and **n't** will be added after the to do verb and to do with **n't** will be placed before the subject in the interrogative sentence.	**Assertive:-** He watches the TV. **Interrogative:-** Doesn't he watch the TV?
4	Subject + never + verb + ext.	to do verb + subject + ever + verb + ext.?	When there is 'never' used in the assertive sentence, to make an interrogative sentence to do verb will be used as Question word and 'never' is replaced by 'ever'.	**Assertive:-** I never play chess. **Interrogative:-**Do I ever play chess?
5	subject + auxiliary verb + verb + nothing + ext.	auxiliary verb + subject + verb + anything + ext.?	When there is 'nothing' used in the assertive sentence, to make it interrogative sentence, sentence starts with auxiliary verb and 'nothing' is replaced by 'anything'.	**Assertive:-** I have nothing to do with it. **Interrogative:-** Do I have anything to do with it?

6	everybody/ all/ everyone + verb + ext.	Who + to do verb + n't + verb + ext.?	When there is everybody/all/ everyone used in the assertive sentence, to make it interrogative sentence, everybody/all/everyone is replaced by **'who + to do verb' and n't** will have to add after the to do verb.	**Assertive:-** Everybody condemns a thief. **Interrogative:-**Who doesn't condemn a thief?
7	Nobody + auxiliary verb +verb+ ext.	Who + auxiliary verb+ verb + ext.? auxiliary verb + anybody + verb+ ext.?	When there is **'Nobody'** used in the assertive sentence, to make it interrogative sentence, 'Nobody is replaced by **'Who'**. When there is 'Nobody' used in the assertive sentence, to make it interrogative sentence, sentence starts with auxiliary verb and 'nobody' is replaced by 'anybody'	**Assertive:-** Nobody can reach the answer accurately. **Interrogative:-**Who can reach the answer accurately? Can anybody reach the answer accurately?
8	none/ no one + auxiliary verb+ verb + ext.	who + auxiliary verb+ verb + ext.? auxiliary verb + anyone + ext.?	When there is **'none/no one** used in the assertive sentence, to make it interrogative sentence, 'none/ no one' is replaced by **'who'**. When there is **none/no one** used in the assertive sentence, to make it interrogative sentence, sentence starts with auxiliary verb and 'none/no' one is replaced by **'anyone'**.	**Assertive:-** None/ No one can touch the ceiling. **Interrogative:-**Who can touch the ceiling? Can any one touch the ceiling?

Transformation Rules - Assertive to Imperative Sentence

S.no	Assertive Sentence structure	Imperative Sentence structure	Tips	Example
1	You + auxiliary verb + verb + ext.	Verb + ext.	When the assertive sentence consists auxiliary verb and no negative word then to make it imperative remove subject and auxiliary verb from sentence.	**Assertive:-** You should exercise daily. **Imperative:-** Do the exercise daily.
2	you +auxiliary verb + not + verb + ext.	Do + not + verb + ext.	When the assertive sentence consists auxiliary verb and negative word 'not' then to make it imperative remove subject and auxiliary verb from sentence and start sentence with 'Do Not'.	**Assertive:-**You do not roam around. **Imperative:-** Do not roam around.

SENTENCE STRUCTURE

3	you + should + never + verb + ext.	Never + verb + ext.	When the assertive sentence consists of auxiliary verb 'should' and negative word 'never', to make it imperative remove subject and auxiliary verb from sentence and start sentence with 'Never'	**Assertive:-** You should never tell a lie. **Imperative:-** Never tell a lie.
4	I/We/He/She/ Noun + verb + ext.	Let + me/ us/ him/ her/ them/ noun + verb + ext.	When the assertive sentence consists of subject other then 'you' and no auxiliary verb then to make it imperative use object form of pronoun if subject is pronoun and start sentence with 'Let'	**Assertive:-** She sings a song. **Imperative:-** Let her sing a song.
5	I/we/he/she/ they/ + auxiliary verb + not + verb + ext.	Let me/ us/ him/ her/ them + not + verb + ext.	If the assertive sentence consist of pronoun as subject other then 'you' and auxiliary verb and also negative word 'not' then to make it imperative use object form of pronoun and start sentence with 'Let' and place 'not' after subject.	**Assertive:-** We do not do it. **Imperative:-** Let us not do it
6	Noun + auxiliary verb + not + verb + ext.	Let not + noun + verb + ext.	When the assertive sentence consists of noun as subject and auxiliary verb and also negative word 'not' then to make it imperative start sentence with 'Let not'.	**Assertive:-** John does not go there. **Imperative:-** Let not John go there.

Transformation Rules - Assertive to Exclamatory Sentence

Sr.no	Assertive Sentence structure	Exclamatory Sentence structure	Tips	Example
1	Subject + verb + a + very + adjective/ adverb + ext.	What + a/ an + adjective/ adverb + ext. + subject + verb!	In exclamatory sentence, a very is replaced by what +a/ an and these are used after verb and before adjective/ adverb.	**Assertive:-** It is a very interesting movie. **Exclamatory:-** What an interesting movie it is!
2	Subject + verb + very + adjective/ adverb + ext.	how + adjective/ adverb + ext. + subject + verb!	In exclamatory sentence, very is replaced by how and it is used after verb.	**Assertive:-** The picture looks very nice. **Exclamatory:-** How nice the picture looks!
3	Subject + wish + subject + verb + ext.	If + subject + verb + ext.!	For subject + wish, if is used in exclamatory sentence.	**Assertive:-** I wish I had walked on the moon. **Exclamatory:-** If I had walked on the moon!

| 4 | Subject + wish + subject + could + verb + ext. | would that + subject + could + verb + ext! | For subject + wish + could, if /would that is used in exclamatory sentence | Assertive:-We wish we could live in that mansion. Exclamatory:- Would that we could live in that mansion! |

Transformation Rules - Exclamatory to Assertive Sentence

Sr.no	Exclamatory Sentence structure	Assertive Sentence structure	Tips	Example
1	what + a/an + adjective/ adverb + subject + verb!	Subject + verb + a + very + adjective/ adverb.	In assertive sentence, what + a/an is replaced by very and these are used after verb and before adjective/ adverb.	Exclamatory:- What a good chef he is! Assertive:- He is a good chef.
2	How + adjective/ adverb + subject + verb!	Subject + verb + very + adjective/ adverb.	In assertive sentence, how is replaced by very and it is used after verb.	Exclamatory:- How nicely you arranged the meeting! Assertive:-You arranged the meeting very nicely.
3	Hurrah! Subject + verb + ext.	It is a matter of joy that + subject + verb + ext.	Hurrah is replaced by it is a matter of joy	Exclamatory:- Hurrah! we have won the debate. Assertive:- It is a matter of joy that we have won the debate.
4	Alas! Subject + verb + ext.	It is a matter of sorrow that + subject + verb + ext.	Alas is replaced by it is a matter of sorrow.	Exclamatory:- Alas! I am disappointed. Assertive:-It is a matter of sorrow that I am disappointed.
5	If + subject + were/ verb(past) + ext.!	Subject + wish + subject + were/ verb(past) + ext.	For 'If were/verb(past)', subject + wish + were/ verb(past) is used in assertive sentence.	Exclamatory:- If I danced with Amanda! Assertive:-I wish I danced with Amanda.

SENTENCE STRUCTURE

6	Were/Had + subject + ext.!	Subject + wish + subject + were/had + ext.	For **'Were/ Had', subject + wish + were/had** is used in assertive sentence.	**Exclamatory:-** Were I a child again!
				Assertive:- I wish I were a child again.
7	Would that + subject + could + verb + ext.!	Subject + wish + subject + could + verb + ext.	For **if /would that subject + wish** is used in assertive sentence.	**Exclamatory:-** Would that we could have a holiday today!
				Assertive:- We wish we could have a holiday today.

Chapter 13 — PUNCTUATION

Punctuations are marks such as full stop, comma and brackets, used in writing to separate sentences and their elements and to clarify meaning. When we speak, we use pauses and the pitch of the voice to express ourselves clearly but in written English, punctuations are vital to disambiguate the meaning of sentences.

For example – *"A new born, without its mother, is nothing."* Here, *the emphasis is on the mother.* *"New born: without it, mother is nothing."* Here, *the emphasis is on the new born.* So, from these two examples, we can understand how punctuations play a significant role in clarifying the meaning of a sentence. Punctuations consist of both rules and conventions which should be followed while writing. Below are some common punctuation marks with their rules and conventions along with examples that will help you understand the usage of punctuation marks in English language.

Full stop (.)

➢ Full stops are used to mark the end of a sentence.

Example

He is a nice person. She works in a sugar mill.

➢ Full stops are also used in initials for personal names.

Example

F.W.Taylor, David M. Joshua

➢ Full stops are also used in abbreviations.

Example

Dr. (doctor), Prof. (professor), R.A.M (Random Access Memory) and W.T.C (World Trade Center) etc.

Question mark (?)

➢ Question marks are used to make clear what is said is a question.

Example

Do you need a mobile phone? Are you coming from the market?

Exclamation mark (!)

➢ Exclamation marks are used to indicate an exclamative clause or expression in informal writing.

PUNCTUATION

Example :
> Listen! Don't go out of the room. Oh my God! We have won the match.

Note: When we want to indicate something shocking or extremely important in informal writing, we use more than one exclamation mark.

Example :
> Oh no!!! I am again late for the office. Oh my gosh!!! He is no more.

Comma (,)

➢ Commas are used to separate a list of similar words or phrases.

Examples :
> He was friendlier, more talkative and more open than last time I met him.
> It is advised to write in simple, clear and accurate words.

➢ We use commas to separate words or phrases that mark where the voice would pause slightly.

Examples :
> I can't tell you now. However, I will tell you tomorrow.
> He has, in fact, lost all his money in gambling.

➢ When main clauses are separated by *and, or, but*, we don't normally use a comma if the clauses have the same subject. However, we sometimes use commas if the clauses have different subjects.

Examples :
> She was very friendly and invited us to her villa in Spain. (Same subject)
> Cricketers these days earn more money but they are fitter and play many more matches. (Same subject)
> It was an expensive gift to buy, but we decided it was worth the money. (Different subjects)

➢ We use commas to separate the clauses when a subordinate clause comes before the main clause. However, we do not always do this in short sentences.

Examples :
> If you get lost in the museum, please don't hesitate to call us.
> If you get lost just call us.

➢ Commas are used to mark non-defining clauses. Such clauses normally add extra, non-essential information about the noun or noun phrase.

Examples :
> The bus, which arrived after ten minutes, took all the children to the picnic.
> India, which has become a technology hub, is a very different country now.

- We commonly separate question tags, yes-no response and 'please' expression with commas.

Examples
- He is a good boy, isn't he?
- Yes, I want to have some coffee.
- Please, shut the door.

- Commas are also used to separate vocatives, discourse markers and interjections.

Examples :
- Pick up the phone, Joseph, can you? Thanks. (Vocative)
- Well, what do you think we should do in the matter? (Discourse marker)
- Great, that sounds really exciting. (Interjection)

- We use commas to show that direct speech is following or has just occurred.

Examples :
- He said, "I am watching a movie".

Note: When the direct speech is first, we use a comma before the closing of the quotation marks. Example – "We will not go", he said impatiently.

Colon (:)

- Colons are used to introduce lists.

Examples :
- There are three main reasons for the success of the Indian Cricket team: correct guidance, hard work and self-belief.

- Colons are also used to indicate a subtitle or to indicate a subdivision of a topic.

Examples :
- 1965: Stories from the Second Indo-Pak War
- The world is a stage: play your role well.

Semi-colon (;)

- We use semi-colons instead of full stops to separate two main clauses. In such cases, the clauses are related in meaning but are separated grammatically.

Examples :
- English is spoken throughout South America; in Brazil, the main language is Portuguese.
- Mary was hurt; she knew he only said it to upset her.

PUNCTUATION

> Semi-colons can replace 'and' or 'but'. They denote a pause that's longer than a comma but shorter than a full stop.

Note: Semi-colons are not commonly used in contemporary English.

Quotation mark ('....' and "....")

> Quotation marks are used in direct speech; we enclose what is said within a pair of single or double quotation marks.

Example :

The teacher said, "Have you all done the homework?" **or**

The teacher said: 'Have you all done the homework?'

> We use single quotation marks to draw attention to a word.

Examples :

I am very disappointed by his 'apology'. I don't think he meant it at all.

> Single quotation marks are also used to refer to the titles of books, newspapers, magazines, movies and poems etc.

Examples :

An interesting article has been published in 'The Times of India'.

'Life of a pie' is an award winning movie.

Dashes (-)

> A dash or hyphen is used to link words together.

Examples

Sub-part, non-verbal, first-class and week-end etc.

Other Punctuation Marks

> We use brackets to make an aside or a point which is not a part of the main flow of the sentence. Even if we remove the words between the brackets, the sentence would still make the same sense.

Examples :

Mahatma Gandhi (father of nation) has written the book 'My experiment with truth'.

Mahatma Gandhi has written the book 'My experiment with truth'.

> The apostrophe (') has two main uses:
>   (1) To indicate possession or ownership.

Examples :

    The boy's watch was beautiful. Ram's mother has come to the school.

    (2) To indicate where a letter is omitted.

Examples:

    I'll come today which means *I will* come today

    The time is *4 o'clock* which means the time is *4 of the clock.*

Note: People usually get confused between 'its' and 'it's'. The examples below will clearly show the difference between these two and their usage.

➢ Use "it's" when you mean it is or it has.

Examples :

    It's a pleasant day.

    It's your right to vote in the election.

    It's been great getting to know you.

➢ Use "its" when you are using it as a possessive.

Examples :

    The dog has hurt its paws.

    The company celebrated its silver jubilee.

    The sugar is in its container.

TIPS AND TECHNIQUES FOR PUNCTUATIONS

There is no short-cut and nothing to mug up in punctuations; all you need to do is read books, newspapers, magazines and good blogs as much as you can so that you get to see plethora of punctuations and their uses in different ways This will help you hone your skills and knowledge of punctuations.

All the rules and conventions mentioned above are very important to keep in mind, so, it is advised that try to write sentences and use lot of punctuations while writing and check them later on whether you have correctly used them or not. Doing this will enable you gain confidence in the usage of punctuations. After following these tips, you will be able to pick wrongly used punctuations just by having a glance over the sentences.

Chapter 14: CONTRACTION

A contraction is an abbreviated version of a word or words made by shortening and combining two words. We make contractions with auxiliary verbs, and also with *be* and *have* when they are not auxiliary verbs. When we make a contraction, we commonly put an apostrophe in place of a missing letter. For example – *can't* (can+not), *don't* (do+not) and *haven't* (have+not) etc.

We use contraction in both speaking and writing; however, these are usually not appropriate in formal writing.

Examples of uses of contractions in sentences:

- He *didn't* go to school yesterday.
- Please, *don't* open the window now.
- I *haven't* eaten.
- *Isn't* he a good boy?
- *Let's* celebrate Arthur's birthday.
- *She'll* do the work before time.
- You *shouldn't* have broken the glass in anger.
- Finally, *we're* going for the picnic.

The following are the most common contractions:

AM		
I am	I'm	I'm a teacher.

ARE		
You are	you're	You're funny.
We are	we're	We're happy.
They are	they're	They're going to the market.
Who are	who're	Who're you?

HAVE		
I have	I've	I've had too much drink.
You have	you've	You've been a good sister.
We have	we've	We've been to London.
They have	they've	They've been on the swings.
Could have	could've	He could've helped the poor boy.
Would have	would've	We would've worn a sweater.
Should have	should've	She should've put on a hat.
Might have	might've	I might've asked for another glass of water.
Who have	who've	Who've you spoken to?
There have	there've	There've been a number of visitors today.

IS, HAS		
He is/ has	he's	He's a nice boy.
She is/ has	she's	She's a nice girl.
It is/ has	it's	It's a pleasant day.
What is/ has	what's	What's for lunch?
That is/ has	that's	That's good news.
Who is/ has	who's	Who's coming tonight?
There is/has	there's	There's no water in the vase.
Here is/has	here's	Here's one apple in the fridge.
One is/has	one's	One's needed to represent our family.

WILL (or SHALL)		
I will	I'll	I'll see you soon.
You will	you'll	You'll be on time, right?
She will	she'll	She'll be late.
He will	he'll	He'll be early.
It will	it'll	It'll be here soon.
We will	we'll	We'll see you later.
They will	they'll	They'll get there first.
That will	that'll	That'll be great.

CONTRACTION

There will	there'll	There'll be lots to see.
This will	this'll	This'll be fun.
What will	what'll	What'll we do?
Who will	who'll	Who'll be there?

WOULD, HAD		
I would/ had	I'd	I'd like a glass of water.
You would/ had	you'd	I wish you'd let me come along with you.
He would/ had	he'd	He'd like a biscuit.
She would/ had	she'd	She'd like milk.
We would/ had	we'd	We'd go there soon.
They would/ had	they'd	They'd like something to drink.
It would/ had	it'd	It'd be troublesome.
There would/ had	there'd	There'd be a little delay.
What would/ had	what'd	What'd you expect?
Who would/ had	who'd	Who'd have known?
That would/ had	that'd	That'd be great.

US		
Let us	let's	Let's help the old man.

Negative Contractions

NOT		
Cannot	can't	I can't come today.
Do not	don't	Don't touch the wire.
Is not	isn't	It isn't safe to drive without a helmet.
Will not	won't	I won't enter the room unless asked.
Should not	shouldn't	I shouldn't go first.

Could not	couldn't	I couldn't be the last one.
Would not	wouldn't	I wouldn't want to be third.
Are not	aren't	Aren't you Manish's cousin?
Does not	doesn't	He doesn't want to come with us.
Was not	wasn't	He wasn't paying attention.
Were not	weren't	They weren't afraid.
Has not	hasn't	He hasn't called yet.
Have not	haven't	I haven't received the mail.
Had not	hadn't	I hadn't thought of that.
Must not	mustn't	I mustn't get too upset.
Did not	didn't	He didn't know what to do at that moment.
Might not	mightn't	I mightn't do it again.
Need not	needn't	You needn't worry about me, I'll be fine.

TIPS & TECHNIQUES FOR CONTRACTIONS

To be frank, there is no short-cut and nothing to mug up in contractions; all you need to do is read books, newspapers and magazines etc. as much as you can so that you get to different contractions and their uses.

Chapter 15: COMMON ERRORS

English grammar is a majorly important part of English section in almost all entrance examinations. A number of students face lot of problems while solving the questions based on common errors because most of the time, they are unaware of the rules of grammar which leads to committing very common mistakes.

To enhance your grammar knowledge and help you overcome committing common mistakes, below are given some examples along with explanations that will be very helpful and handy to you.

➢ Only I and my friend were at the concert. (WRONG)

Only my friend and I were at the concert. (RIGHT)

(Pronouns order – **I** and **me** come last when more than one pronoun is used in a phrase, **you** comes next to last, and **third-person** pronoun comes first.)

➢ Everybody will get their share. (WRONG)

Everybody will get **his** share. (RIGHT)

('Everybody' may sound like 'a lot of people', but it is a singular noun and takes a singular verb.)

➢ Most of the students found difficult to comprehend his speech. (WRONG)

Most of the students found **it** difficult to comprehend his speech. (RIGHT)

➢ Don't pride on your victory. (WRONG)

Don't pride **yourself** on your victory. (RIGHT)

(Without the reflexive pronoun 'yourself', it would be impossible for the reader to know who you pride on.)

➢ I have a good news for you. (WRONG)

I have good news for you. (RIGHT)

('News' is uncountable, which means that not only it is followed by a singular verb, but you also cannot say 'a news').

➢ The boys leave the school at five o'clock. (WRONG)

The boys leave school at five o'clock. (RIGHT)

(Daily routine, not leaving for any specific purpose)

- They realized where their weak points were and how to get rid of them. (WRONG)

  They realized where their weak points were and how **they could** get rid of them (RIGHT)

  (A fragment with a missing subject; hence, an appropriate subject to form an independent clause should be included.)

- While doing the work, there are obstacles ahead. (WRONG)

  While doing the work, **they met with** obstacles. (RIGHT)

  (Needs to revise a dangling modifier by naming the appropriate doer of the action as the subject of the main clause.)

- He cannot set a foot in my house. (WRONG)

  He cannot **set foot in** my house. (RIGHT)

  (The idiom is 'set foot in' and not 'set a foot in')

- Andamans are a group of islands. (WRONG)

  The Andamans are a group of islands. (RIGHT)

  ('The' is used with the places consisting many islands; for example – The Bahamas, The Maldives, The Philippines and The West Indies etc.)

- She pretended to not recognize the man in the market. (WRONG)

  She pretended not to recognize the man in the market. (RIGHT)

- She neither speaks English nor French. (WRONG)

  She speaks neither English nor French. (RIGHT)

  (Here, 'neither' modifies the verb 'speak' whereas, it should modify the language 'English'.)

- Fire broke out in our neighbourhood. (WRONG)

  A fire broke out in our neighbourhood. (RIGHT)

  (While fire, as a substance, is uncountable, but 'a fire broke out' gives a mental image of a single fire.)

- His heart sank and could hardly stand. (WRONG)

  His heart sank and **he** could hardly stand. (RIGHT)

  (A fragment with a missing subject; hence, an appropriate subject to form an independent clause should be included.)

COMMON ERRORS

- All I know is my friend is right. (WRONG)

  All I know is that my friend is right. (RIGHT)

  (Here, the verb 'is' connected with reporting can be followed by a that-clause acting as the direct object.)

- He has not yet gone to the bed. (WRONG)

  He has not yet gone **to bed**. (RIGHT)

  ('Go to bed' means to lie down to sleep, to put oneself in one's bed while 'go to the bed' means not necessarily preparing for sleep.

- I saw him to play. (WRONG)

  I saw **him play**. (RIGHT)

  (Here, use of the preposition 'to' is inappropriate. There are two patterns of this kind of sentences: 1) I saw him play = I saw him play throughout the game. 2) I saw him playing = I saw him on the field but I don't know whether he actually finished the action.)

- The answer of this question is not so easy. (WRONG)

  The answer to this question is not so easy. (RIGHT)

  (The answer to the question is the normal grammatical form like key to the problem.)

- Water composes of hydrogen and oxygen. (WRONG)

  Water **is composed** of hydrogen and oxygen. (RIGHT)

  ('Be composed' of something means to be formed from various things like, air is composed mainly of nitrogen and oxygen.)

- I didn't see him too. (WRONG)

  I didn't see him either. (RIGHT)

  ('Either' is used in negative sentences to add an agreeing thought: Tom doesn't speak French. Sam doesn't speak French either.)

- The polar bear is not used to live in hot places. (WRONG)

  The polar bear is not **used to living** in hot places. (RIGHT)

  ('Be used to' is followed by a noun (or pronoun) or the gerund – the 'ing' form of a verb like, I can't get used to getting up early.)

- Nobody is bound to suffering. (WRONG)

  Nobody is **bound to suffer**. (RIGHT)

  ('Bound' after verb + 'to' infinitive means certain or extremely likely to happen like, you're bound to forget people's name often.)

COMMON ERRORS

- Have you read the Shakespeare's Macbeth? (WRONG)
  Have you read Shakespeare's Macbeth? (RIGHT)
- She rarely goes to theatre. (WRONG)
  She rarely goes **to the theatre**. (RIGHT)
  ('The', the definite article is used because you're talking about something 'definite'.)
- Adams invited me to a party. (WRONG)
  The Adams invited me to a party. (RIGHT)
  (If you are referring some members of a family, you make it plural by adding 'the' in the beginning.)
- Shiela felt sorry about the street children but she did not voice. (WRONG)
  Shiela felt sorry about the street children but she did not voice it. (RIGHT)
  (The sentence is incomplete without the objective case 'it'.)
- He was astonished by her sudden resignation. (WRONG)
  He was astonished **at** her sudden resignation. (RIGHT)
  (If you are astonished by something, you are very surprised about it: I was astonished by his stupidity. Here, contextual use is 'at'.)
- The judge has decided the case. (WRONG)
  The judge has decided **upon the case.** (RIGHT)
  (To make a judgement about some aspect of someone or something; 'Upon' is formal and less commonly used than on.)
- Do you want to try these new skates? (WRONG)
  Do you want to try out these new skates? (RIGHT)
  ('Try out' means 'to undergo a competitive qualifying test; to test or use something experimentally').
- Tom's project is more perfect than Sam's. (WRONG)
  Tom's project is **better than/superior to** Sam's. (RIGHT)
  (There are words like 'square' and not 'more square' or round and not 'more round' similarly, it is perfect, unique or not unique etc.)
- This machine cost me hundred dollars. (WRONG)
  This machine cost me **a hundred dollars.** (RIGHT)
  (If you spell out dollars, it would be usual to also spell out a hundred or one hundred: You owe me a hundred dollars or you owe me $100.)

COMMON ERRORS

- He has good knowledge of Zoology. (WRONG)
  He has **a good knowledge** of Zoology. (RIGHT)
- French are industrious and frugal. (WRONG)
  The French are industrious and frugal. (RIGHT)
  (French means of, relating to, or characteristic of France or its people or culture; The French denotes people of France or the natives/inhabitants of France collectively.)
- David has just been commissioned as the captain. (WRONG)
  David has just been commissioned **as captain**. (RIGHT)
- He will be great help for you. (WRONG)
  He will be of great help to you. (RIGHT)
  ('Of great help to you should be used as it is grammatically correct.)
- Both of them did not win the election. (WRONG)
  Neither of them won the election. (RIGHT)
  (Additive phrases (both, also, too, etc.) are not used when overall meaning of them is to negate.)
- He told that he would be visiting Father on weekend. (WRONG)
  He said that he would be visiting Father on weekend. (RIGHT)
  (Use 'tell' with a personal object and 'said' when there is no personal object.)
- Hardly the sun had risen when we set out. (WRONG)
  Hardly had the sun risen when we set out. (RIGHT) or
  The sun had **hardly** risen **when** we set out. (RIGHT)
  (If hardly, scarcely, barely and no sooner are in the initial position, the subject and auxiliary are inverted: Hardly had we arrived home when the doorbell rang or we had hardly arrived home when the doorbell rang.)
- Not only she speaks English but also Chinese. (WRONG)
  She speaks **not only English** but also Chinese. (RIGHT)
  (For proper parallel structure, the verb following the subject must precede 'not only' so that it applies to both parallel phrases – English and Chinese.)
- Suppose, if she arrives late, you will miss the train. (WRONG)
  Suppose she arrives late, you will miss the train. (RIGHT)
  (Use suppose, supposing and what if + present verb form to make suggestions about what might happen. **Suppose and if do not come together.**)

COMMON ERRORS

- He did good in the exams. (WRONG)
  He did well in the exams. (RIGHT)
  (Good is an adjective and a verb cannot be modified by an adjective. Well is an adverb and it goes after the verb or verb + object.)
- It was bitter cold that night. (WRONG)
  It was bitterly cold that night. (RIGHT)
  ('Cold' itself is an adjective; hence, can be modified by an adverb 'bitterly' and not by adjective i.e. 'bitter')
- The movie is too interesting. (WRONG)
  The movie is very interesting. (RIGHT)
  ('Too' means more than enough; do not use in the sense of very or much.)
- No one writes as neat as Susan does. (WRONG)
  No one writes as neatly as Susan does. (RIGHT)
  ('Neat' is an adjective which can't modify a verb i.e. 'write'; 'neatly' meaning 'with neatness' is an adverb which correctly modifies the verb 'write'.)
- The grandmother is living miserly. (WRONG)
  The grandmother is living in a miserly way. (RIGHT)
  (Not all words ending in -ly are adverbs like miserly is an adjective.)
- The receptionist sat on her desk. (WRONG)
  The receptionist sat **at** her desk. (RIGHT)
- Everybody must conform with the rules. (WRONG)
  Everybody must **conform to** the rules. (RIGHT)
  ('Conform' means to comply with rules, standards, or laws'; conform to hygiene regulations; in some special usages 'conform with' is used: changes have to conform with international classifications.)
- The Himalayas are covered by snow. (WRONG)
  The Himalayas are covered **with/in** snow. (RIGHT)
  'Covered by' usually means that the covering actually hides the thing that is covered)
- Divide the apple in four parts. (WRONG)
  Divide the apple **into** four parts. (RIGHT)
  (To or cause to separate into parts or groups: divide students into small discussion groups; Book divided into various chapters etc.)

COMMON ERRORS

- This is an exception of the rule. (WRONG)
  This is an **exception to** the rule. (RIGHT)
- My leg is paining. (WRONG)
  There's/I've got a pain in my leg. (RIGHT)
  (Use pain as noun and precede it by have or feel.)
- They behaved cowardly. (WRONG)
  They behaved **in a cowardly manner**. (RIGHT)
  (Cowardly, silly and miserly are all adjectives which can't modify verbs)
- A 80% majority agree to the decision made by the principal. (WRONG)
  A 80% majority agrees to the decision made by the principal. (RIGHT)
  (Here, the word 'majority' is used for a collective group, hence, it should be treated as singular.)
- She does not know swimming. (WRONG)
  She does not know to swim. (RIGHT)
- Open your book on page 15. (WRONG)
  Open your book **at** page 15. (RIGHT)
- She died from Cancer. (WRONG)
  She died **of** Cancer. (RIGHT)
- He lives besides my house. (WRONG)
  He lives beside my house. (RIGHT)
  (Besides and beside have different meanings. Beside shows position whereas besides means 'in addition'.)
- I have lost my patience. (WRONG)
  I have lost patience. (RIGHT)
- You have no influence on him. (WRONG)
  You have no influence **over** him. (RIGHT)
- He insisted to go there. (WRONG)
  He insisted **on** going there. (RIGHT)
- We reached safely. (WRONG)
  We reached safe. (RIGHT)

- ➢ There were less people. (WRONG)
  There were fewer people. (RIGHT)
- ➢ He had no other alternative. (WRONG)
  He had no alternative. (RIGHT)
- ➢ He shouted not as loud as the rest of the people. (WRONG)
  He shouted not as loudly as the rest of the people. (RIGHT)
  (The adverb 'loudly' should be used.)
- ➢ Verbal orders shall not be obeyed. (WRONG)
  Oral orders shall not be obeyed. (RIGHT)
  (Use of the adjective verbal is inappropriate in the context of the sentence.
- ➢ You have paid the bill, isn't it? (WRONG)
  You have paid the bill, haven't you) (RIGHT)
- ➢ Varun threatened to divorce her often. (WRONG)
  Varun often threatened to divorce her. (RIGHT)
  (If you put a modifier in a different place in the sentence, it means something different.)
- ➢ You should learn how to cope up. (WRONG)
  You should learn how to cope. (RIGHT)
- ➢ There is nothing such as luck. (WRONG)
  There is no such thing as luck. (RIGHT)
- ➢ The maid almost washed all of the utensils. (WRONG)
  The maid washed almost all of the utensils. (RIGHT)
  (You should be very careful in placing the adverb in the sentence as it has a different meaning.)
- ➢ After the party, I will return to my quarter. (WRONG)
  After the party, I will return to my **quarters**. (RIGHT)
- ➢ It is more cold now. (WRONG)
  It is **colder** now. (RIGHT)
  (The comparative adjective 'colder' should be used).
- ➢ He was late for office and fired by his boss. (WRONG)
  He was late for office and was fired by his boss. (RIGHT)
  (Parallel verb phrase 'was' should be used)

COMMON ERRORS

TIPS AND TECHNIQUES IN COMMON ERRORS

➤ Read the sentence all the way through. Even if you think the error is in part B, make sure to read the entire sentence as this will help prevent you from falling into traps.

➤ Always check for subject-verb agreement. The verb needs to take a form that matches the subject.

➤ You are not done only by picking the error because it sounds weird or because it's not the word you would use. You should be able to explain to yourself what error the answer you picked contains. If you can't do so, it's probably not the right choice.

➤ Lastly, read English newspapers and articles etc. as much as you can so that you get accustomed to English language. Reading habits, many times, help you pick the errors just by having a glance over the sentence.

VOCABULARY

Chapter 16 VOCABULARY

A set of all the words that exist in a particular language or subject is vocabulary. Learning vocabulary is a very important part of learning a language. The more words you know, the more you will be able to understand what you hear and read; and the better you will be able to say what you want to speak or write. In this chapter, various sections like Synonyms, Antonyms, Analogies, Homophones and Foreign words and Expression etc. have been given to enhance your vocabulary which will help you in the coming examinations.

One word – A small collection

Abdicate – Renounce a throne or high office

Accomplice – One associated with another especially in wrong-doing

Acoustics – Science of the production, transmission, reception and effects of sound

Actuary – One who calculates insurance and annuity premium etc.

Amnesty – General pardon

Abattoir – A building where animals are killed for meat

Agnostic – One who believes that nothing can be known about God

Alimony – Compensatory allowance given to wife after divorce

Altruist – One who is habitually kind to others

Anecdote – A short interesting or amusing story

Backwater – A part of river out of the main stream, where the water does not move

Barbecue – A metal flame on which meat etc. is cooked over an open fire

Bibliography – A list of writings on a subject

Biennial – Happening once every two years

Blue blood – The quality of being a noble person by birth

Bonsai – The art of growing a plant in a pot that is prevented from reaching its natural size

Boulevard – A broad street having trees on each side

Bourgeois – Belonging to the middle class

Bric-a-brac – Small object kept for decoration

VOCABULARY

Bullion – Bars of Gold or Silver

Cabal – A small group of people who make secret plans for political action

Cannibal – One who eats human flesh

Catch-22 – A situation from which one is prevented from escaping by something that is part of the situation itself.

Charlatan – One who deceives others by falsely claiming to have a skill

Celibacy – One who does not indulge in carnal pleasure

Cloak-and-Dagger – Stories that deal with adventure and exciting mystery

Coagulate – Change from a liquid into a solid by chemical action

Colonnade – A row of pillars supporting a roof or arches

Consortium – A combination of several companies, banks etc. for a common purpose

Contretemps – An unlucky and unexpected event, socially uncomfortable position with someone

Defeatism – the practice of thinking in a way that shows an expectation of being unsuccessful

Deja vu – The feeling of remembering something that in fact one is experiencing for the first time

Dragnet – A system of connected actions and methods for caching criminals

Dregs – Sediment in a liquid that sinks to the bottom and is thrown away

Drudgery – Hard uninteresting work

Dally – Waste time

Dawdle – Take one's time; proceed slowly

Dearth – An insufficient quantity or number

Demeanor – The way a person behaves toward other people

Diffident – Lacking self-confidence

Enigmatic – That which is mysterious and very hard to understand

Empirical – Based on practical experience of the world we see and feel

Entomology – The scientific study of insects

Epicurean – Lover of physical/material

Egalitarian – Favouring social equality

Expressionism – A style of painting which expresses feelings rather than describing objects and experiences

Enamor – Attract

Ennui – The feeling of being bored by something tedious

Epoch – A period marked by distinctive character
Exculpate – Pronounce not guilty of criminal charges
Febrile – Of or caused by fever
Felony – A serious crime such as murder or armed robbery
Fluvial – Of, found in, or produced by rivers
Foible – A small rather strange and stupid personal habit
Foray – A sudden rush into enemy country
Freckle – A small flat brown spot on the skin
Fumigate – To clear of disease, bacteria etc. by means of chemical smoke
Feign – Give a false appearance of
Founder- Walk with great difficulty
Forlorn – Marked by or showing hopelessness
Graffiti – Drawing or writing on a wall
Grange – A large country house with farm buildings
Guinea pig – A person who is subject of some kind of test
Gentry – The most powerful members of a society
Germane – Relevant and appropriate
Gibberish – Unintelligible talking
Gibe – An aggressive remark directed at a person
Gird – Prepare oneself for action or a confrontation
Gloat – Dwell on with satisfaction
Gripe - Complain
Halitosis – A condition in which one has bad health
Headstrong – Determined to do what one wants in spite of all advice
Heirloom – A valuable object passed on for generations
Hinterland – The inner part of a country
Hothead – One who does things too quickly, without thinking
Haggle – An instance of intense argument (as in bargaining)
Helm – A position of leadership
Hireling – A person who works only for money
Humongous – Very large
Hoard – Save up as for future use
Idolatry – The worship of idols

VOCABULARY

Implacable – Impossible to satisfy, change, or make less angry
Incorporeal – Without a body or form
Innate – Being talented through inherited qualities
Inseminate – To put male seed into a female
Intelligentsia – Those who are highly educated and often concern themselves with ideas and new developments
Intestate – Not having made a will
Invective – A forceful attacking speech used for blaming someone
Imperious – Having or showing arrogant superiority
Impromptu – Without advance preparation
Juxtapose – To place side by side or close together
Jaded – Bored or apathetic after experiencing too much of something
Jaunt – A journey taken for pleasure
Jaunty – Having a cheerful, lively, and self-confident air
Jeer - Laugh at which contempt and derision
Jejune – Lacking interest or significance or impact
Jeopardize – Pose a threat to; present a danger to
Jest – Activity characterized by good humour
Jettison – Throw away, of something encumbering
Jibe – An aggressive remark directed at a person
Ken – Range of what one can know or understand
Kindle – Cause to start burning
Knave – A deceitful and unreliable scoundrel
Knoll – A small natural hill
Kimono – A long loose garment made of silk
Kudos – An expression of approval and commendation
Killjoy – Someone who spoils the pleasure of others
Knack – A special way of doing something
Kindred – Group of people related by blood or marriage
Kleptomaniac – Someone with an irrational urge to steal
Lackey – One who behaves like a servant by always obeying
Labile – Readily undergoing change or breakdown
Lachrymose – Showing sorrow
Lacklustre – Lacking brilliance or vitality

Laconic – Brief and to the point
Lament – Express grief verbally
Languor – A feeling of lack of interest or energy
Leery – Openly distrustful and unwilling to confide
Lethargic – Deficient in alertness or activity
Limpid – Clear and bright
Malady – Any unwholesome or desperate condition
Malcontent – One who is dissatisfied with the existing state of affairs
Misnomer – A name wrongly or mistakenly applied
Morbid – Having or expressing a strong interest in sad or unpleasant things
Malleable – Easily influenced
Manumit – Free from slavery or servitude
Maudlin – Effusively or insincerely emotional
Maul – Injure badly
Melancholy – Characterized by or causing or expressing sadness
Melee – A noisy riotous fight
Namesake – A person or thing that has the same name as another
Necromancy – The practice which claims to learn about the future by talking with the dead
Nemesis – Just and unavoidable punishment
Newfangled – New (idea or machine etc.) but neither necessary nor better
Nihilism – The belief that nothing has meaning or value
Nadir – The lowest or most unsuccessful point in a situation
Narcissist – Someone who is excessively self-centered
Nefarious – Extremely wicked
Nestle – Move or arrange oneself in a comfortable and cosy position
Nether – Lower
Obtrude – To be pushed or push oneself into undue prominence
Obviate – To clear away or provide for, as an objection or difficulty
Odoriferous – Having a smell
Ostracism – The state of not being included in a group
Obdurate – Showing unfeeling resistance to tender feelings
Oblique – Not direct, explicit, or straightforward
Obloquy – State of disgrace resulting from public abuse

VOCABULARY

Obsolete – No longer in use

Obtuse – Slow to learn or understand; lacking intellectual acuity

Ogle – Look at with amorous intentions

Panacea – A solution or remedy for all difficulties or diseases

Panache – Being able to do things in a confidant and elegant way

Panegyric – A speech or a piece of writing praising somebody or something

Perdition – A state of eternal punishment and damnation into which an unrepentant person passes after death

Perjury – A lie told on purpose in court

Placate – Make someone less angry or hostile

Platonic – A friendly, not sexual, relationship between a man and a woman

Plebeian – Of the lower social class

Portend – Be a sign or warning that (something, especially something momentous or calamitous) is likely to happen

Putsch – A sudden secretly planned attempt to remove a government by force

Quixotic – Trying to do the impossible, often so as to help others, while getting oneself into danger

Quadruped – An animal especially a mammal having four limbs

Quaff – To swallow hurriedly or greedily or in one draught

Quaint – Attractively old-fashioned

Qualm – Uneasiness about the fitness of an action

Quandary – A situation from which extrication is difficult

Quash – Put down by force or intimidation

Quell – Suppress or crush completely

Quibble – Argue over petty things

Quirk – A strange attitude or habit

Raconteur – One who is good at telling stories in an interesting way

Recumbent – Lying down on the back or side

Rescind – To make void, as an act, by the enacting authority or by a superior authority

Retribution – A justly deserved penalty

Rancour – A feeling of deep and bitter anger and ill-will

Ravenous – Extremely hungry

Rebuke – An act or expression of criticism and censure

Recoil – Draw back as with fear or pain
Refurbish – Make brighter and prettier
Relegate – Assign to a lower position
Sapient – Wise and full of deep knowledge
Snippet – A short piece from something spoken or written
Souvenir – An object kept as a reminder of something
Stoic – One who is indifferent to joys or sorrows
Stratagem – A trick to deceive an enemy
Superannuated – Too old for work
Surreal – Having a strange dreamlike unreal quality
Sardonic – Disdainfully or ironically humorous
Satiate – Fill to satisfaction
Spurn – Reject with contempt
Transient – Lasting only for a short time
Tacit – Implied by or inferred from actions or statements
Taciturn – Habitually reserved and uncommunicative
Tantamount – Being essentially equal to something
Taper – Diminish gradually
Temerity – Fearless daring
Terse – Brief and to the point
Threshold – The entrance for passing through a room or building
Throng – A large gathering of people
Toil – Work hard
Underling – A person of low rank in relation to another
Ubiquitous – Being present everywhere at once
Ultimatum – A final peremptory demand
Umbrage – A feeling of anger caused by being offended
Uncanny – Surpassing the ordinary or normal
Unctuous – Unpleasantly and excessively suave or ingratiating
Underscore – Give extra weight to
Unfledged – Young and inexperienced
Unfounded – Without a basis in reason or fact
Unison – The act of occurring together or simultaneously

VOCABULARY

Valise – A small bag used while travelling
Vacillate – Be undecided about something
Vacuous – Devoid of intelligence
Vagary – An unexpected and inexplicable change in something
Vainglorious – Feeling self-importance
Valour – Great courage in the face of danger, especially in battle
Vanity – The trait of being unduly conceited
Vanquish – Come out better in a competition, race, or conflict
Vantage – Place or situation affording some benefit
Vapid – Lacking significance or liveliness or spirit or zest
Weakling – One who lacks physical strength or strength of character
Wretch – An unfortunate or unhappy person
Waggish – Witty or joking
Waif – A homeless child especially one forsaken or orphaned
Wail – A cry of sorrow and grief
Waive – Do without or cease to hold or adhere to
Wallow – Devote oneself entirely to something
Wane – A gradual decline (in size/strength/power/number)
Waver – Be unsure or weak
Weary – physically and mentally fatigued
Xenophobia – Fear of strange or foreign people and customs etc.
Yearn – Desire strongly or persistently
Yahoo – A person who is not intelligent or intelligent in culture
Yelp – A sharp high-pitched cry
Yeoman – A free man who cultivates his own land
Yoke – Become joined or linked together
Yokel – A person who is not intelligent or interested in culture
Yonder – Distant but within sight
Yore – Time long past
Yuppie – A young man in a professional job with a high income
Yell – A loud, sharp cry of pin, surprise or delight
Zeitgeist – The intellectual and moral tendencies that characterize any age or epoch
Zany – Ludicrous or foolish

Zeal – A feeling of strong eagerness
Zealot – A fervent and even militant proponent of something
Zealous – Marked by active interest and enthusiasm
Zenith – The point above the observer directly opposite the nadir
Zephyr – A slight wind
Zest – Vigorous and enthusiastic enjoyment
Zonk – Hit or strike

Foreign words and phrases

Foreign words and phrases are generally not asked directly. But the knowledge of foreign words and phrases will help you in reading comprehension and other types of common questions. So, make yourself familiar with the common foreign words and phrases.

- **Ab initio** : from the beginning.
- **Addenda** : 'list of additions'. (addenda to a book)
- **Ad valorem** : according to value.
- **Ad infinitum** : to infinity.
- **A la carte** : according to the bill of fare. (a la carte dishes are available)
- **Alter ego** : the other self, intimate friend, (Kissinger was the alter ego of Nixon)
- **Amende honorable** : satisfactory apology, reparation.
- **Amour propre** : self love
- **Ancien regime** : a political or social system that has been displaced by another.
- **A posteriori** : empirical
- **A priori** : from cause to effect, presumptive. (every science cannot be taught a priori)
- **Apropos** : in respect of
- **An couran** : fully acquainted with matters.
- **Au fait** : completely familiar with
- **Au revoir** : until we meet again (to say au revoir at parting)
- **Avant propos** : preliminary matter, preface
- **Beau ideal** : the ideal of perfection.
- **Beaumonde** : the world of fashion.
- **Beaux esprits** : men of wit.

VOCABULARY

- **Bete noire** : a special aversion (Uncle Symond was my father's bête noire)
- **Bon voyage** : a good voyage or journey to you
- **Casus belli** : that which causes or justifies war.
- **Cause celebre** : a celebrated or notorious case in law
- **Charge d' affaires** : diplomat inferior in rank to an Ambassador but acting on his behalf in his absence.
- **Chef d' oeuvre** : masterpiece (Mona Lisa is Vinci's Chef-d' oeuvre)
- **Circa** : about ('circa 1930')
- **Contretemps** : an unexpected or untoward event; a hitch
- **Corrigenda** : a list of errors (in a book)
- **Coup d'etat** : violent change in government.
- **Coup de grace** : a finishing stroke. (The coup de grace of the Russian Revolution was the total annihilation of the Czar family)
- **Cul-de-sac** : a blind alley (The failure of the Policy of non-alignment in 1962 saw our foreign policy reach a cul-de-sac)
- **De facto** : actual or actually (de facto recognition to a state)
- **Dejure** : from the law, by law.
- **Denovo** : anew, again (trial of a case)
- **Denouement** : the end of a plot (in play)
- **De profundis** : out of the depths
- **Dernier resort** : last resort
- **Detente** : easing of strained relations especially between states / countries
- **Dramatis personae** : characters of a drama or play
- **Enfant terrible** : a terrible child; one who makes disconcerting remarks
- **En rapport** : in harmony
- **Entourage** : friends, group of people accompanying a dignitary.
- **Errata** : list of errors
- **Esprit de corps** : the animating spirit of a collective body, as a regiment.
- **Eureka** : a cry of joy or satisfaction when one finds or discovers something.

- Ex-officio : in virtue of his office.
- Expose : a statement
- Expost facto : acting retrospectively
- Fait accompli : a thing already done.
- Faux pas : a false step; slip in behaviour
- Hoi polloi : the rabble, ordinary people
- Inextenso : unextended small in extension
- Ipso facto : by that very fact.
- Laissez faire : non interference
- Mal-a-propos : ill-timed
- Mutatis mutandis : with the necessary changes (rules will come into force mutatis mutandis)
- Noblesse oblige : rank imposes obligation.
- Nota bene : note well
- Par excellence : pre-eminently.
- Pari passu : side by side.
- Per se : by itself.
- Piece de resistance : the main dish of a meal.
- Poste restante : to remain in the post office till called for. (said of letters)
- Pro bone publico : for the good of the public
- Protégé : one under the protection of another. (S.Vietnam is US's protege).
- Quid pro quo : an equivalent, something in return.
- Raisond'etre : the reason for a thing's existence.
- Sanctum sanctorum : holy of holies. (temple, church etc.)
- Seiratim : in a series
- Sub rosa : under the rose; confidentially
- Sui gereris : in a class by itself
- Summon bonum : the chief good.
- Terra incognita : an unknown country
- Tour deforce : a notable feat or strength of skill.
- Ultra vires : beyond one's authority
- Vox populi, vox die : The voice of the people is The voice of God.
- Zeitgeist : spirit of the age

VOCABULARY

One word with different meanings

Multiple meaning words are those which we use for different meanings in different contexts. The same word can be used as noun, adjective or verb etc. Below is list of some common words that have different meanings.

1. Ream
   - A pile of paper
   - To juice a citrus fruit
2. Mean
   - Average
   - Not nice
3. Tender
   - Gentle
   - To pay money
4. Harbour
   - A sheltered area of water that is deep enough so that ships can anchor there
   - To provide shelter
5. Hatch
   - The process of a baby bird coming out of its egg
   - An opening in the floor, ceiling, or wall of a ship or aircraft
6. Caper
   - A pickled flower bud used to flavour food
   - A prank, or a playful activity for amusement
7. Carp
   - A type of fish
   - To find fault or complain about small matters
8. Flake
   - A small particle or piece of something
   - To become flabby or languid
9. Nick
   - A small cut or small notch
   - To steal (slang)
10. Page
    - A sheet of paper, on one side of it, in a book
    - A boy who acts as a servant, sometimes wearing a uniform.

Homophones

A homophone is a word which is pronounced the same as another word but differs in meaning. Below are given few examples of homophones.

Air, Heir	Lead, Led
Allowed, Aloud	Loan, Lone
Alter, Altar	Made, Maid
Ate, Eight	Peace, Piece
Band, Banned	Pain, Pane
Bean, Been	Pair, Pear
Blew, Blue	Raise, Rays
Brake, Break	Sight, Site
Cell, Sell	Tail, Tale
Ceiling, Sealing	Throne, Thrown
Check, Cheque	Steal, Steel
Coarse, Course	Son, Sun
Die, Dye	Tide, Tied
Groan, Grown	To, Too, Two
Hair, Hare	Vain, Vane, Vein
Hall, Haul	Waist, Waste
Heel, Heal	We, Wee
Knew, New	Wait, Weight

Synonyms and Antonyms

A synonym is a word that means exactly or nearly the same as another word or phrase in the same language, for example – *shut* is a synonym of *close*. An antonym is a word opposite in meaning to another word, for example – *bad* is an antonym of *good*.

Following are some words and against each word are given the list of Synonyms and Antonyms separately:

➤ Allure
Synonym: Tempt, Entice, Fascinate
Antonym: Repulse, Deter, Repel, Distaste

➤ Apparent
Synonym: Distinct, Evident, Obvious, Perceptible
Antonym: Obscure, Indistinct, Masked, Doubtful

➤ Axiom
Synonym: Maxim, Truth, Saying, Dictum
Antonym: Blunder, Absurdity, Irrelevant, Ridiculousness

➤ Astute
Synonym: Clever, Intelligent, Wise, Brilliant
Antonym: Dull, Shallow, Unintelligent, Solid

VOCABULARY

- Abash
Synonym: Discourage, Confound, Embarrass, Discompose
Antonym: Encourage, Uphold, Hearten, Embolden
- Bleak
Synonym: Dismal, Gloomy, Chilly, Dreary
Antonym: Bright, Pleasant, Cheerful, Balmy
- Brittle
Synonym: Frail, Fragile, Breakable, Delicate
Antonym: Tough, Enduring, Strong, Unbreakable
- Benevolence
Synonym: Humanity, Generosity, Charity, Liberality
Antonym: Malevolence, Inhumanity, Malignity, Unkindness
- Barbarous
Synonym: Savage, Uncivilized, Untamed, Brutal
Antonym: Cultured, Humane, Refined, Gentle
- Bewitching
Synonym: Magical, Fascinating, Tantalising, Spell binding
Antonym: Repulsive, Repugnant, Nauseating, Disgusting
- Corpulent
Synonym: Obese, Ugly, Fat, Awkward
Antonym: Thin, Slim, Lean, Delicate
- Consternation
Synonym: Fear, Disappointment, Dismay, Hopelessness
Antonym: Repose, Peace, Calm, Fearless
- Concede
Synonym: Yield, Assent, Permit, Sanction
Antonym: Reject, Deny, Dissent, Disallow
- Commodious
Synonym: Convenient, Suitable, Roomy, Comfortable
Antonym: Inconvenient, Unsuitable, Uncomfortable, Confined
- Chastise
Synonym: Punish, Admonish, Scold, Reprove
Antonym: Cheer, Comfort, Encourage, Stimulate
- Despicable
Synonym: Contemptible, Worthless, Shameless, Base
Antonym: Worthy, Decent, Honourable, Respectable
- Disdain
Synonym: Detest, Despise, Scorn, Loathe
Antonym: Approve, Praise, Love, laud
- Defray
Synonym: Meet, Bear, Spend, Pay
Antonym: Decline, Declaim, Refuse, Abjure

- Dainty
Synonym: Elegant, Delicate, Refined Exquisite
Antonym: Clumsy, Coarse, Unpleasant, Insipid
- Deplore
Synonym: Lament, Bemoan, Complain, Regret
Antonym: Cheer, Rejoice, Applaud, Celebrate
- Exult
Synonym: Brag, Triumph, Rejoice, Applaud
Antonym: Lament, Deplore, Bemoan, Grieve
- Equivocal
Synonym: Uncertain, Vague, Hazy, Ambiguous
Antonym: Lucid, Obvious, Clear, Plain
- Encumbrance
Synonym: Hindrance, Burden, Obstacle, Impediment
Antonym: Incentive, Stimulant, Patronize, Vantage
- Earnest
Synonym: Ardent, Sincere, Resolute, Determined
Antonym: Unheeding, Frivolous, Negligent, Careless
- Enjoin
Synonym: Direct, Counsel, Exhort, Command
Antonym: Prohibit, Forbid, Revolt, Dissuade
- Fabricate
Synonym: Construct, Produce, Build, Manipulate
Antonym: Destroy, Wreck, Dismantle, Demolish
- Frantic
Synonym: Violent, Agitated, Frenzied, Wild
Antonym: Subdued, Gentle, Lucid, Coherent
- Fleeting
Synonym: Transient, Temporary, Ephemeral, Transitory
Antonym: Enduring, Perpetual, Eternal, Unceasing
- Fickle
Synonym: Wavering, Unreliable, Unsteady, Volatile
Antonym: Resolute, Determined, Inalterable, Invariable
- Feud
Synonym: Strife, Quarrel, Row, Contention
Antonym: Fraternity, Harmony, Reconciliation, Recompose
- Guile
Synonym: Cunning, Deceit, Duplicity, Chicanery
Antonym: Honesty, Frankness, Sincerity Integrity
- Grisly
Synonym: Disgusting, Atrocious, Monstrous, Loathsome
Antonym: Pleasing, Beautiful, Attractive, Alluring

VOCABULARY

- Gaudy

Synonym: Garish, Brilliant, Glittering, Tawdry
Antonym: Dull, Faded, Sober, Solemn

- Genial

Synonym: Cheerful, Pleasant, Joyful, Affable
Antonym: Sullen, Dismal, Morose, Melancholy

- Grudge

Synonym: Hatred, Aversion, Unwilling, Objection
Antonym: Benevolence, Affection, Goodwill, Kindness

- Hustle

Synonym: Hurry, Bustle, Haste, Activity
Antonym: Quiet, Lull, Idle, Motionless

- Haughty

Synonym: Arrogant, Pompous, Obstinate, Imperious
Antonym: Humble, Submissive, Modest, Inoffensive

- Hapless

Synonym: Unfortunate, Ill-fated, Hostile, Doomed
Antonym: Fortunate, Lucky, Favoured, Satisfied

- Haggard

Synonym: Exhausted, Emaciated, Lean, Gaunt
Antonym: Exuberant, Active, Robust, Lively

- Heretic

Synonym: Nonconformist, Secularist, Dissident, Offender
Antonym: Conformable, Adaptable, Religious, Believer

- Intimidate

Synonym: Frighten, Dictate, Hopeless, Irresolute
Antonym: Console, Encourage, Appease, Hearten

- Intrepid

Synonym: Brave, Courageous, Valorous Chivalrous
Antonym: Scared, Frightened, Timid, Cowardly

- Innocuous

Synonym: Salutary, Wholesome, Innocent, Harmless
Antonym: Deleterious, Baneful, Insanitary, Injurious

- Impute

Synonym: Attribute, Ascribe, Charge, Indict
Antonym: Exculpate, Support, Excuse, Vindicate

- Indigence

Synonym: Privation, Destitution, Insolvency, Penury
Antonym: Affluence, Abundance, Opulence, Luxury

- Just

Synonym: Honest, Impartial, Righteous, Upright
Antonym: Unfair, Unequal, Discriminatory, Unseasonable

VOCABULARY

- Jubilant

Synonym: Rejoicing, Triumphant, Gay, Cheerful
Antonym: Melancholy, Depressing, Gloomy, Despondent

- Jovial

Synonym: Frolicsome, Cheerful, Merry, Exultant
Antonym: Morose, Solemn, Malcontent, Sad

- Jaded

Synonym: Tired, Exhausted, Fatigued, Languish
Antonym: Renewal, Recreation, Restoration, Refreshed

- Jejune

Synonym: Dull, Boring, Uninteresting, Monotonous
Antonym: Interesting, Exciting, Piquant, Thrilling

- Kindred

Synonym: Relation, Species, Relative, Affinity
Antonym: Unrelated, Dissimilar, Heterogeneous, Disparate

- Keen

Synonym: Sharp, Eager, Acute, Poignant
Antonym: Vapid, Insipid, Blunt, Undesiring

- Knave

Synonym: Dishonest, Scoundrel, Vagabond, Rogue
Antonym: Paragon, Innocent, Benefactor, Idealist

- Knell

Synonym: Death knell, Last blow, Demolish, Suppress
Antonym: Reconstruction, Rediscovery, Procreation, Resurrection

- Knotty

Synonym: Complicated, Difficult, Arduous, Onerous
Antonym: Simple, Manageable, Tractable, Flexible

- Luscious

Synonym: Palatable, Delicious, Delectable, Delightful
Antonym: Unsavoury, Tart, Sharp, Sour

- Luxuriant

Synonym: Profusion, Abundant, Dense, Plentiful
Antonym: Scanty, Meagre, Inadequate, Deficient

- Lucid

Synonym: Sound, Rational, Sane, Coherent
Antonym: Obscure, Hidden, Incomprehensible, Unintelligible

- Linger

Synonym: Loiter, Prolong, Hesitate, Delay
Antonym: Hasten, Quicken, Dart, Hurry

- Languid

Synonym: Pensive, Lethargic, Exhausted, Fatigued
Antonym: Lively, Animated, Refreshed, Restored

VOCABULARY

- Mutinous
Synonym: Recalcitrant, Insurgent, Unruly, Revolutionary
Antonym: Submissive, Faithful, Complaint, Loyal
- Murky
Synonym: Dusky, Dreary, Dismal, Bleak
Antonym: Bright, Shining, Luminous, Radiant
- Mollify
Synonym: Appease, Assuage, Relieve, Mitigate
Antonym: Irritate, Aggravate, Infuriate, Exasperate
- Mettle
Synonym: Courage, Determination, Stamina, Spirit
Antonym: Timidity, Fear, Cowardice, Diffident
- Mendacity
Synonym: Falsehood, Deception, Perjury, Perfidious
Antonym: Probity, Honesty, Veracity, Candour
- Noxious
Synonym: Baneful, Injurious, Pernicious, Disastrous
Antonym: Healing, Profitable, Innocuous, Salubrious
- Nimble
Synonym: Prompt, Brisk, Lively, Agile
Antonym: Sluggish, Languid, Weary, Tardy
- Nullify
Synonym: Cancel, Annual, Obliterate, Invalidate
Antonym: Confirm, Uphold, Empower, Endorse
- Nauseous
Synonym: Unsavoury, Loathsome, Abominable, Repellent
Antonym: Worthy, Commendable, Upright, Inoffensive
- Novice
Synonym: Tyro, Beginner, Debutant, Apprentice
Antonym: Veteran, Ingenious, Experienced, Mentor
- Overwrought
Synonym: Excited, Agitated, Fervent, Intense
Antonym: Quiet, Tranquil, Composed, Cool
- Oversight
Synonym: Omission, Error, Fault, Slip
Antonym: Precision, Observance, Circumspection, Caution
- Ostentation
Synonym: Display, Pretension, Vaunt, Pomposity
Antonym: Modesty, Constraint, Diffidence, Economy
- Odious
Synonym: Abhorrent, Obnoxious, Prejudice, Malevolent
Antonym: Engaging, Fascinating, Endearing, Captivating

- Obstinate
Synonym: Stubborn, Resolute, Unyielding, Obdurate
Antonym: Submissive, Obedient, Amenable, Pliable
- Puerile
Synonym: Shallow, Immature, Childish, Trivial
Antonym: Wise, Farsighted, Profound, Sensible
- Prudent
Synonym: Cautious, Discreet, Judicious, Circumspect
Antonym: Impetuous, Unwise, Reckless, Rash
- Protract
Synonym: Prolong, Delay, Stretch, Procrastinate
Antonym: Abbreviate, Curtail, Abridge, Compress
- Pillage
Synonym: Ransack, Ravage, Despoil, Plunder
Antonym: Recompense, Recover, Redeem, Restoration
- Pompous
Synonym: Haughty, Arrogant, Flamboyant, Florid
Antonym: Unpretentious, Humble, Coy, Modest
- Quell
Synonym: Subdue, Reduce, Suppress, Extinguish
Antonym: Exacerbate, Agitate, Foment, Instigate
- Quaint
Synonym: Queer, Strange, Odd, Ridiculous
Antonym: Familiar, Usual, Common, Normal
- Quibble
Synonym: Equivocate, Prevaricate, Evade, Dissemble
Antonym: Unfeigned, Plain, Scrupulous, Conscientious
- Quash
Synonym: Abrogate, Annual, Cancel, Revoke
Antonym: Uphold, Empower, Authorize, Permit
- Quarantine
Synonym: Isolate, Separate, Seclude, Screened
Antonym: Gregarious, Amiable, Sociable, Companionable
- Rustic
Synonym: Pastoral, Bucolic, Rural, Uncivilised
Antonym: Cultured, Refined, Urban, Urbane
- Rout
Synonym: Defeat, Overthrow, Vanquish, Subjugate
Antonym: Succumb, Withdraw, Retreat, Consolidate
- Rescind
Synonym: Annual, Abrogate, Revoke, Repeal
Antonym: Delegate, Permit, Authorize, Propose

VOCABULARY

- Repugnant
Synonym: Hostile, Offensive, Disagreeable, Distasteful
Antonym: Agreeable, Pleasant, Friendly, Tasteful
- Raze
Synonym: Demolish, Destroy, Annihilate, Dismantle
Antonym: Restore, Construct, Repair, Build
- Sway
Synonym: Influence, Control, Command, power
Antonym: Impotence, Futility, Disability, Incapacity
- Sycophant
Synonym: Parasite, Flatterer, Cringing, Servile
Antonym: Devoted, Loyal, Truthful, Faithful
- Subvert
Synonym: Overthrow, Suppress, Demolish, Sabotage
Antonym: Accomplish, Sustain, Generate, Organize
- Squalid
Synonym: Dirty, Soiled, Filthy, Odious
Antonym: Attractive, Tidy, Polished, Spruce
- Saucy
Synonym: Impudent, Insolent, Brazen, Impertinent
Antonym: Modest, Humble, Esteem, Meek
- Trivial
Synonym: Trifling, Insignificant, Frivolous, Worthless
Antonym: Significant, Important, Consequential, Essential
- Throng
Synonym: Assembly, Gathering, Congregation, Crowd
Antonym: Dispersion, Scattering, Handful, Sparsely
- Trite
Synonym: Ordinary, Commonplace, Stale, Hackneyed
Antonym: Interesting, Extraordinary, Becoming, Proper
- Temerity
Synonym: Boldness, Audacity, Imprudence, Indiscretion
Antonym: Discretion, prudence, Caution, Wisdom
- Taciturn
Synonym: Reserved, Uncommunicative, Silent, Reticent
Antonym: Talkative, Loquacious, Garrulous, Extrovert
- Utterly
Synonym: Completely, Entirely, Extremely, Wholly
Antonym: Deficient, Incomplete, Insufficient, Partial
- Usurp
Synonym: Seize, Wrest, Encroach, Coup
Antonym: Restore, Compensate, Reinstate, Grant

- Unseemly
Synonym: *Undesirable, Inappropriate, Uncouth, awkward*
Antonym: *Becoming, Acceptable, Decorous, Admirable*
- Ungainly
Synonym: *Clumsy, Unskilled, Immature, Slovenly*
Antonym: *Active, Expert, Skilful, Dexterous*
- Uncouth
Synonym: *Awkward, Ungraceful, Inelegant, Vulgar*
Antonym: *Elegant, Graceful, Distinguished, Shapely*
- Vouch
Synonym: *Confirm, Consent, Approve, Endorse*
Antonym: *Repudiate, prohibit, Recant, Retract*
- Vicious
Synonym: *Corrupt, Obnoxious, Degraded, Demoralized*
Antonym: *Noble, Virtuous, Innocent, Undefiled*
- Vanity
Synonym: *Conceit, Pretension, Immodesty, Pride*
Antonym: *Modesty, Humility, Meek, Bashful*
- Valour
Synonym: *Bravery, Prowess, Heroism, Chivalry*
Antonym: *Fear, Cowardice, Unmanliness*
- Valiant
Synonym: *Brave, Gallant, Courageous, Chivalrous*
Antonym: *Fearful, Afraid, Coward, Dastardly*
- Wary
Synonym: *Cautious, Circumspect, Prudent, Chary*
Antonym: *Heedless, Negligent, Impulsive, Reckless*
- Withhold
Synonym: *Reserve, Restrain, Hamper, Retard*
Antonym: *Emancipate, Liberate, Dispense, Release*
- Wane
Synonym: *Decline, Dwindle, Decrease, Deteriorate*
Antonym: *Ameliorate, Rise, Revive, Wax*
- Wayward
Synonym: *Volatile, Capricious, Unstable, Inconstant*
Antonym: *Stable, Determined, Resolute, Straight*
- Wilful
Synonym: *Stubborn, Obstinate, Obdurate, Inexorable*
Antonym: *Amenable, Irresolute, Pliable, Yielding*
- Yawn
Synonym: *Gape, Sleepy, Slumber, Doze*
Antonym: *Active, Close, Brisk, Wakeful*

VOCABULARY

➤ Yoke
Synonym: Connect, Harness, Hitch, Shackle
Antonym: Liberate, Release, Detach, Disconnect
➤ Yield
Synonym: Surrender, Abdicate, Succumb, Consent
Antonym: Resist, Protect, Prohibit, Forbid
➤ Yell
Synonym: Shout, Shriek, Exclaim, Gesticulate
Antonym: Suppress, Whisper, Muffled, Muted
➤ Yearn
Synonym: Languish, Crave, Require, Pine
Antonym: Content, Unwanted, Satisfied, Gratified
➤ Zest
Synonym: Delight, Enthusiasm, Energetic
Antonym: Disgust, Passive, Detriment, Languid
➤ Zigzag
Synonym: Oblique, Crooked, Winding, Wayward
Antonym: Straight, Even, Direct, Unbent
➤ Zenith
Synonym: Summit, Apex, Maximum, Pinnacle
Antonym: Nadir, Base, Floor, Bottom
➤ Zeal
Synonym: Eagerness, Fervour, Enthusiasm, Ardour
Antonym: Apathy, Lethargy, Indifference, Reluctant
➤ Zealot
Synonym: Fanatic, Partisan, Bigot, Chauvinist
Antonym: Tolerant, Liberal, Blasphemy, Impious

Spelling Errors

Questions based on English spelling errors are asked in many exams. At times, we commit mistakes by choosing the wrong option considering it to be the right spelling of the word as we are in habit of using the wrongly spelt words since we started writing English. Spellings can be tricky because spellings are not based on phonetics and also because there are many exceptions.
Below is a table of some incorrect words with their correct spellings. You should read and analyze them thoroughly so that you do not commit mistake while writing.

INCORRECT	CORRECT
Abscence	Absence
Accomodate	Accommodate
Arguement	Argument

VOCABULARY

Assasination	Assassination
Athiest	Atheist
Attendence	Attendance
Bizzare	Bizarre
Calender, Calander	Calendar
Commitee	Committee
Concious	Conscious
Convinient	Convenient
Copywrite	Copyright
Deterioreit	Deteriorate
Embarass	Embarrass
Explaination	Explanation
Foreward	Foreword
Foriegn	Foreign
Fourty	Forty
Grammer	Grammar
Guidence	Guidance
Heros	Heroes
Hypocracy	Hypocrisy
Interupt	Interrupt
Lollypop	Lollipop
Managable	Manageable
Mispell	Misspell
Neice	Niece
Noticable	Noticeable
Occured	Occurred
Opthamologist	Ophthalmologist
Pavillion	Pavilion
Persue	Pursue
Posession	Possession

VOCABULARY

Preceeding	Preceding
Priviledge	Privilege
Pronounciation	Pronunciation
Que	Queue
Questionaire	Questionnaire
Reccomend	Recommend
Rediculous	Ridiculous
Rythm	Rhythm
Seige	Siege
Seperate	Separate
Sincerly	Sincerely
Supercede	Supersede
Tatoo	Tattoo
Tendancy	Tendency
Tommorrow	Tomorrow
Tounge	Tongue
Truely	Truly
Untill	Until
Vaccum	Vacuum
Vegeterian	Vegetarian
Wierd	Weird
Yachet	Yacht

Analogies

Analogy, literally means a comparison or a comparable similarity. A student has to find a pair of words in the same relation or a similar relation as that of the given pair of words. Analogy is, in a sense, a test of vocabulary since you need to know the meaning of the words given, but in a broader sense, it is a test of reasoning ability. To know the meaning of the words will not be enough if one is not able to understand clearly what the relation between the pairs of words is. Therefore, there are two things that are important to attempt a question on analogy:
(i)   meaning of all given words
(ii) relationship between the given pairs of words

VOCABULARY

It is more convenient and time saving to first figure out the relation between the given pair and then compare it with the relations between the pairs in the options given for choice. Consider the following example

Pen : Write : : Book : ?

Now, first determine the relation between the first two words, it is that of purpose, pen is used to write. Then determine the other word which will be in the same relation to the third word. Book is used to read, then

Pen : Write : : Book : Read

There are different kinds of relationships that could be drawn from daily usage but some common relationships are given below:

1. CAUSE : EFFECT
   Liquor : Intoxication → Liquor causes intoxication
   Wound : Pain → wound causes pain.
   In this relation, the first word is the cause for the second and the second is the result of the first

2. PURPOSE
   Bottle : Cork → a cork is used to close a bottle
   Dress : Cloth → cloth is used to make a dress
   In this relation, one word is used for another i.e. there is a purpose between the two

3. OBJECT : ACTION
   Gun : Fire → you fire a gun
   Violin : Play → you play a violin
   In this, one term is an object and the other one is an action undertaken with the help of that object.

4. ACTION : OBJECT
   Foment : Riot → you foment a riot
   Wear : Clothes → you wear clothes
   This is opposite to the previous relation. Here, the first word is the action and the second the object with which that action is done.

5. PART : WHOLE
   Book : Literature → a book is a part of the larger body of literature
   Ship : Fleet → ship is a part of the collection called fleet
   In this relation, the first word will in the same way be a constituent of a bigger body represented by the second word.

6. SYNONYMS
   Abundant : Ample → ample means the same as abundant
   Skilled : Adroit → the two words are synonymous, i.e., they mean the same
   This relation is when both the words are synonyms.

7. ANTONYMS :
   Abstinence : Indulgence → Indulgence means the opposite of Abstinence
   Legitimate : Unlawful → Legitimate means legal which is the opposite of unlawful.
   In this relation, the two words are opposite to each other in meaning.

VOCABULARY

8. **SECONDARY SYNONYMS :**
    Callous : Indifference → The synonym of callous will be indifferent, since both words are adjectives but rather the noun form, indifference, has been given in the relation
    Brainwave: Inspired → The synonym of Brainwave is inspiration, but instead the second word in this relation is Inspired - the one who has inspiration.
    In this relation, the two words are not directly synonymous but a slight change of the part of speech has been made in the second word.

9. **WORKER: ARTICLE CREATED**
    Carpenter : Furniture → carpenter makes wooden furniture
    Compose : Music → a composer composes or creates music
    In this relation, the first word is the doer and the second is the professional work done by the first.

10. **SYMBOL : QUALITY**
    Olive leaf : Peace → an olive leaf is a symbol of peace.
    Red : Passion → the colour red symbolises passion.
    In this relation the first word is a symbol, and the second is the meaning represented by the symbol.

11. **CLASS : MEMBER**
    mammal : Man → man belongs to the class of mammals.
    Doggerel : Poem → Doggerel is a class of poem which is bad in quality.
    In this relation the first word is a member belonging to the class denoted by the second word.

12. **ACTION : SIGNIFICANCE**
    Blush : Embarrassment → if one blushes, that signifies that the person is embarrassed.
    Spasm : Pain → a spasm indicates that the person is in pain.
    In this relation, the first word is an action and the second is what that action signifies.

Although, most of the questions asked in a competitive exam can be solved with the help of the given relationships, for subtle questions, a student should apply reasoning to figure out the relation between the given words. Following are certain tips that would help a student to attempt analogy questions.

 TIP 1

The first and foremost step while attempting an analogy question should be to define the relationship. To avoid any errors, first define the relationship on paper or in your mind before searching for options. Once you have defined the relationship analyse the given pairs in the light of the relationship.

(1) ANXIOUS : REASSURANCE
→ resentful : gratitude
→ perplexed : classification
→ insured : imagination
→ vociferous : suppression
First, the relationship can be defined as 'need' i.e. an anxious person needs reassurance and then you can check the given pairs to find out that 'a perplexed person needs classification'. Thus, this will be the right analogy.

(2) SIMMER : BOIL
→ Cook : Fry
→ Chill : Freeze
→ Roast : Stew
→ Slice : Cut
Now, establish the relation between the two given words. It is that of degree. Simmer is the lower degree of boil. Just as chill is the lower degree of freeze.

☞ TIP 2

Always be careful about apparent and easy similarity. These are only to deceive the student as you would be attracted by these options. Always confirm all the options and be highly careful while considering an obvious answer.

e.g. STUTTER : SPEECH
→ Blare : hearing
→ Aroma : smelling
→ Astigmatism : sight
→ Novocaine : Touch
Stutter is a defect of speech, so the relation between the two is that of defect. But Blare and hearing are closely related since blare means a harsh sound. This may attract the student, but this is not a relation of defect. This relation is in the third option, astigmatism is a defect of sight. So, always avoid giving into the temptation of obviously correct answers.

☞ TIP 3

Sometimes, a word has two meanings, while what may first come to your mind will be the more frequent use of that word. If you cannot find a logical relation between the two words. Go beyond the obvious meaning and link the word with the other meaning of the second word.

VOCABULARY

MAROON : SAILOR
→ Red : Ship
→ Crimson : Flower
→ Stranded : Tourist
→ Colour : Dress

Maroon also has two meanings the colour 'maroon' and the verb maroon which means being left alone or abandoned. Obviously the second meaning will make a logical relation with sailor, a sailor is marooned just as a tourist is stranded.

TIPS AND TECHNIQUES FOR VOCABULARY

- Read regularly from a variety of sources like newspapers, magazines and blogs etc. as this habit will help you learn new words as well usages of words in different contexts.
- Make a target of learning a new word daily. This technique is used by many people and they have successfully enhanced their vocabulary.
- You should play word games like – Crossword puzzles, Anagrams, Word jumbles and Scrabbles etc. This method will help you discover new words.
- Engage yourself in talking with people in English whenever you get an opportunity so that you may practice the words that you have learnt. Apart from this, it will also help you learn new words during the conversation and in addition help you enhance your fluency in spoken English.

READING COMPREHENSION

Chapter 17
OBJECTIVE COMPREHENSION

Reading Comprehension contains a lot of questions in almost all competitive examinations and thus, it is very important to attempt the questions of this section. Reading comprehension is the most favoured section in English because it doesn't require prior knowledge to solve RCs (Reading Comprehensions). Greater chances of high accuracy in it act as a game changer in clearing the cut off in English section.

In this chapter, we will discuss some tips and techniques to easily approach RCs with high accuracy.

- You need to have ample RCs practice on computer to pass this section with flying colours because while attempting RCs online, you can't underline important points and mark different areas in the passage and therefore, you need to hone your skills by practising regularly.
- Quickly skim through the passage before you read the passage thoroughly or attempt the questions.
- Before you start reading the passage, go through the questions that need to be answered. This will give you a fair idea about what the passage talks about. Once you start reading the passage, you can start locating the answers to questions.
- It is very important to make inferences while reading the passage because most of the questions are not asked directly. Your understanding of the passage and its theme is of utmost importance as it helps you to eliminate the wrong options and pick the right one.
- Before reading the entire passage, first, read the first and last paragraph of the RC to have an idea what the author is saying in the paragraph. This will help you in having an overview of the whole passage.
- When you are attempting a question based on phrase, just read the two-three lines above and below that phrase to have an idea what is implicit from that phrase.

OBJECTIVE COMPREHENSION

- If there are questions on vocabulary then you should attempt them first as it is quite easy to pick the antonyms and synonyms. You don't have to answer the questions in the order they appear to you because in the exams, you have option to skip the questions and move to the next one and again come back to the previous ones as per your choice.
- In most of the cases, elimination of choices works better than selection of choices. You should try to eliminate those options which are broad, narrow, odd and irrelevant to the question asked. This strategy will help you reach the correct choice easily along with high accuracy.
- Mark the answers only if you are sure of it and make sure you don't go for wild guess.
- Never use your past knowledge about the topic to answer any question.
- Read articles in newspapers on regular basis to improve your reading speed and vocabulary.

Examples:

DIRECTIONS (QS. 1 - 10): Read the following passage carefully and answer the questions given below it. Certain words/ phrases have been printed in bold to help you locate them while answering some of the questions.

The Indian education sector is one of the largest sunrise sectors contributing to the country's economic and social growth. The Indian education system, considered as one of the largest in the world, is divided into two major segments of core and non-core businesses. While, schools and higher education form the core group, the non-core business consists of pre-schools, vocational training and coaching classes. The education sector in India is evolving, led by the **emergence** of new niche sectors like vocational training, finishing schools, child-skill enhancement and e-learning. India has emerged as a strong potential market for investments in training and education sector, due to its favourable demographics (young population) and being a services-driven economy. Indian education sector's market size in Financial Year, 2012-13 estimated to be USD 71.2 billion is expected to increase to USD 109.8 billion by Financial Year 2015-2016 due to the expected strong demand for quality education. The market grew at a CAGR of 16.5% during Financial Year 2015-2016.

Education has been made an important and integral part of the national development efforts. The tremendous increase in the number of students and of educational institutions has given rise to the term 'education explosion'. No doubt, this has resulted in serious problems such as inadequacy of financial resources and infrastructure and **dilution** of personal attention to the education and character-formation of the students. Also, there is the unwanted side-effect of enormous increase in the number of educated unemployed. However, we cannot overlook the advantages of education explosion in India. Mere increase in the percentage of literate people does not indicate a qualitative change in the educational standards of the people and a substantial improvement in manpower resources of India. Unemployment problem in India cannot be blamed on the availability of large masses of educated people in India. Uncertainty and vacillation have marked the government's policy regarding the medium of education in India. While the government policy in this respect has not changed, a significant increase in the number of schools-primary and secondary-imparting education through the English medium is a significant development. Thousands of nursery schools that have mushroomed since the last decade **purport** to impart education to infants through English. This is an unwanted development which has been **deprecated** by educationalists and political leaders. Regarding the medium of instruction in colleges and universities, many State Governments have already decided, in principle, to switch over to the regional language. However, the implementation in this respect has remained very slow.

Today, virtually, every university in India is offering correspondence courses for different degrees and diplomas. In fact, correspondence education has opened new vistas for the educational system which could not successfully meet the challenging problem of providing infrastructure for multitudes of new entrants into the portals of higher education. The public demand for higher education was initially met through evening colleges; now correspondence education has come to the rescue of the worried education administrators.

OBJECTIVE COMPREHENSION

1. Which of the following facts is not true regarding the Indian education sector as per the passage?
   (a) It is still in the process of development.
   (b) It is one of the contributors to India's growth.
   (c) There has been a recent trend towards the adoption of regional languages as the medium of instruction.
   (d) Mushrooming of schools imparting English education has been appreciated.
   (e) The number of educated unemployed has increased.

2. As per the passage, India's education system has been able to attract investments because of
   A. The demographic factor.
   B. The Indian economy being service-driven.
   C. Indian democratic governance being an attractive issue.
   (a) Only A   (b) Only B
   (c) Only C   (d) Both A and B
   (e) Both B and C

3. As per the passage, which of the following explains the term 'education explosion'?
   A. Huge investment in the education sector.
   B. Pro-active government policy towards the education sector.
   C. Spurt in the number of students and educational institutions.
   (a) Both A and B   (b) Only C
   (c) Both B and C   (d) Only B
   (e) All of the above statements are correct

4. Which of the following can be inferred from the passage?
   A. Increase in literacy level signifies a qualitative increase in educational attainment of people.
   B. Literacy levels are closely related to improvement in manpower resources.
   C. The existence of educated people does not necessarily contribute to the problem of unemployment.
   (a) Only A   (b) Only B
   (c) Only C   (d) Both A and B
   (e) All A, B and C

5. According to the passage, which of the following statement(s) is/are correct?
   (a) Increase in English medium schools is a welcome sign for the Indian education sector.
   (b) Increase in English medium schools in India is an insignificant, though wanted development.
   (c) Correspondence education has proved to be a panacea in terms of educating people without proper infrastructure.
   (d) The implementation of regional languages as medium of instruction has been quite fast.
   (e) The prospects for future growth of India's education sector look bleak.

6. Which of the following statements cannot be said to be the highlights of the passage?
   A. India's education sector is marked by increase in the number of educated people paralleled by simultaneous growth in unemployment.
   B. There are both positive and negative aspects of the education explosion in India.
   C. The government policy towards education has been that of clarity marked by sincere efforts.

   (a) Only A   (b) Only B
   (c) Only C   (d) All A, B and C
   (e) None of these

DIRECTIONS (Q.7-8): Choose the word which is most similar in meaning to the words printed in bold as used in the passage.

7. Dilution
   (a) Thickening   (b) Concentration
   (c) Extension   (d) Diminution
   (e) Development

8. Emergence
   (a) Disappear   (b) Rise
   (c) Abandonment   (d) Fall
   (e) Lessening

OBJECTIVE COMPREHENSION

DIRECTION (Qs.9-10): Choose the word which is most opposite in meaning to the words printed in bold as used in the passage.

9. Deprecate
   - (a) Derogate
   - (b) Frown
   - (c) Object
   - (d) Commend
   - (e) Disparage
10. Purport
    - (a) Insignificant
    - (b) Connotation
    - (c) Acceptation
    - (d) Intention
    - (e) Purpose

ANSWERS & EXPLANATION

1. (d) All the sentences except sentence D are correct. It is clearly mentioned in the second last paragraph that thousands of nursery schools that have mushroomed since the last decade is an unwanted development which has been deprecated by educationalists and political leaders.
2. (d) It is clearly mentioned in the first paragraph as "India has emerged as a strong potential market for investments in training and education sector, due to its favourable demographics (young population) and being a services-driven economy."
3. (c) 'Education explosion' as mentioned in the paragraph means a tremendous rise in the number of educational institutions and students.
4. (c) Option (c) can be inferred from the second paragraph where it says that unemployment problem in India can't be blamed on the availability of large masses of educated people in India.
5. (c) Option (c) can be inferred from the last paragraph where it says that correspondence education has opened new vistas for the education system which could not be met earlier because of the challenges of providing necessary infrastructure for it.
6. (c) Option (a) and (b) are clearly mentioned in the passage. Option (c) is contradictory to the lines mentioned in the second last paragraph where it says that uncertainty and vacillation have marked the government policy towards medium of education in India.
7. (d) Dilution means weakening in force, content or value. Diminution means reduction is size, content or importance.

8. (b) Emergence means the process of becoming visible or coming into existence or prominence. Rise means to move from lower position to higher position or go up.
9. (d) Deprecate means to express disapproval. Commend means to praise or approve.
10. (d) Purport used as a verb in the passage means to claim, profess or pretend falsely. Intention in general is clear as expressed.

NEW PATTERN READING COMPREHENSION

DIRECTIONS (1-5): Read the following passage divided into number of paragraphs carefully and answer the questions that follow it.

Paragraph 1: Judiciary has become the centre of controversy, in the recent past, on account of the sudden 'Me' in the level of judicial intervention. The area of judicial intervention has been steadily expanding through the device of public interest litigation. The judiciary has shed its pro-status-quo approach and taken upon itself the duty to enforce the basic rights of the poor and vulnerable sections of society, by progressive interpretation and positive action. The Supreme Court has developed new methods of dispensing justice to the masses through the public interest litigation.

Paragraph 2: Former Chief Justice PN. Bhagwat, under whose leadership public interest litigation attained a new dimension comments that "the Supreme Court has developed several new commitments. It has carried forward participative justice. It has laid just standards of procedure. It has made justice more accessible to citizens". The term 'judicial activism' is intended to refer to, and cover, the action of the court in excess of, and beyond the power of judicial review. From one angle it is said to be an act in excess of, or without, jurisdiction. The Constitution does not confer any authority or jurisdiction for 'activism' as such on the Court.

Paragraph 3: Judicial activism refers to the interference of the judiciary in the legislative and executive fields. It mainly occurs due to the non-activity of the other organs of the government. Judicial activism is a way through which relief is provided to the disadvantaged and aggrieved citizens. Judicial activism is providing a base for policy making in competition with the legislature and executive. Judicial activism is the rendering of decisions, which are in tune with the temper and tempo of the times.

Paragraph 4: In short, judicial activism means that instead of judicial restraint, the Supreme Court and other lower courts become activists and compel the authority to act and sometimes also direct the government regarding policies and also matters of administration.

OBJECTIVE COMPREHENSION

Paragraph 5: Judicial activism has arisen mainly due to the failure of the executive and legislatures to act. Secondly, it has arisen also due to the fact that there is a doubt that the legislature and executive have failed to deliver the goods. Thirdly, it occurs because the entire system has been plagued by ineffectiveness and inactiveness. The violation of basic human rights has also led to judicial activism. Finally, due to the misuse and abuse of some of the provisions of the Constitution, judicial activism has gained significance.

1. What does the author want to convey in Paragraph 1?
   (I) Certain personal issues and agendas in recent past in the level of judicial intervention have put a question mark on the credibility of the apex court.
   (II) The Supreme Court is very concerned about the under-privileged sections of the society and thus, has come up with an innovative idea to dispensing justice.
   (III) Public Interest Litigation is a boon for the poor and vulnerable sections of the society as far as the enforcement of their basic rights is concerned.
   (a) Only (I)   (b) Only (II)
   (c) Both (II) and (III) (d) All (I), (II) and (III)
   (e) None of these

2. What is the meaning of the sentence 'From one angle, it is said to be an act in excess of, or without jurisdiction' in the context of paragraph 2?
   (I) Judicial activism can be exercised by the Supreme Court as it is beyond the power of judicial review.
   (II) Judicial activism does not find any mention in the constitution as far as its authority or jurisdiction is concerned.
   (III) The constitution has not limited the authority or jurisdiction to 'activism' hence, it can be exercised over the courts as per the say of the Supreme Court.
   (a) Only (I)   (b) Only (II)
   (c) Only (III)   (d) Both (II) and (III)
   (e) Both (I) and (II)

3. What can't be said about judicial activism in accordance to paragraph 3?
   (a) It emerges when the legislative and the judiciary do not do justice with their work.
   (b) It has the right to put question mark on the legislative and executive part of the government.
   (c) It is exercised in accordance with the demand of the situation.
   (d) It has given the citizenry ample power to demand for their rights from the judiciary.
   (e) It is giving a foundation for policy making in competition with the other organs of the government.

4. Which of the following statements does not relate to Paragraph 5?
   (a) Violation of basic human rights has led to judicial activism.
   (b) There is a suspicion on the executive and the legislative organ of the government as far as their working is concerned.
   (c) Judicial activism has carried forward participative justice thereby justifying that the entire system has been plagued by ineffectiveness and inactiveness.
   (d) Some of the constitutional provisions have been misused.
   (e) The failure of the other organs of the government has led to the emergence of judicial activism.

5. What does the author mean by the phrase 'judicial restraint' in Paragraph 4?
   (I) The limiting of the exercise of their own power by the courts.
   (II) The restriction of power which Supreme Court can impose on other lower courts.
   (III) The liberation of judicial power of the Supreme Court and other courts.
   (a) Only (I)   (b) Only (II)
   (c) Only (III)   (d) Both (I) and (II)
   (e) All (I), (II) and (II)

ANSWER KEY

1. (e)
2. (b)
3. (d)
4. (c)
5. (a)

PARAJUMBLES

Chapter 18
REARRANGING WORDS OR SENTENCES

Parajumbles is the lexical term used for the kind of questions wherein the sentences of a paragraph are jumbled and the examinee is required to figure out the logical sequence of the sentences that would render the paragraph meaningful and grammatically correct.

Such questions basically pertain to rearrangement of a given set of sentences. At times, instead of sentences of a paragraph, phrases of a complex sentence may be jumbled for the candidate to arrange logically.

I. Let us first discuss the single sentence with its parts jumbled.
   THINGS TO BEAR IN MIND/ STRATEGIES TO EMPLOY:
   1. Every sentence has a subject and a predicate. So, locating the **subject** will give headway in arranging the parts of the sentence sequentially. The subject of a sentence is a noun or a pronoun.
   2. **Nouns** are always mentioned first and later get replaced by **pronouns**.
      e.g. Raman told Mona that he trusted her.
         (noun)   (noun)   (pronoun)   (pronoun)
      Heena promised herself that she would not lie again.
         (noun)   (pronoun)   (pronoun)
   3. The predicate contains the verb of the subject. So, locate the verb.
   4. A sentence may be either in **active** or in **passive** voice. In the active voice, the sentence follows the structure, subject+verb+object+preposition.
      e.g. Adit helped them in their work.
         (subject) (verb) (object)
      In the passive voice, the 'by phrase' containing the doer of the action occurs towards the end of the sentence
      e.g. They were helped in their work *by Adit.*
      or at the end of a clause with correlative conjunction.
      e.g. She was *so* spoilt *by her parents that* she threw tantrums every now and then.

5. **Connectors** occur generally in the middle or alternatively, in the beginning of the sentence.

   e.g. **If** you are happy, you will be healthy.

   You will be healthy **if** you are happy.

   That he is ill is no news.

   It is no news **that** he is ill.

6. Definite article **the** comes later to refer to the noun already mentioned. As an opener, it can come only with singularly known nouns like sun, moon, monuments, newspapers, trains etc.

EXAMPLES

Example 1.

   P: where Gandhi Ji stood

   Q: our long discussions about socialism

   R: had left me

   S: rather bewildered and confused as to just

   (a) PSQR   (b) QRSP
   (c) SPQR   (d) PSRQ

Step 1. Looking for the subject

Observing the parts, we can eliminate R and S as they are parts of the predicate. So, option c) is ruled out. If we take P is the opening part, it may be followed by R and S but Q doesn't fit in the sequence. So, options a) and d) get eliminated. Therefore, the opening part, containing the subject, will be Q.

Step 2. Arranging the predicate

Q may be followed by R or S.

The sequence QRSP makes good, complete sense.

The sequence QSP... is unable to include R.

Therefore, the sequence QRSP which is option b) is the correct one.

Example 2.

1: which is essential for its complete understanding

2: the five page introduction to the script places it in the right perspective

3: and gives the uninitiated reader

REARRANGING WORDS OR SENTENCES

4: a background to the film

    (a) 3214   (b) 2341

    (c) 1324   (d) 4231

Step 1. Locating the subject

Parts 1 and 3 are eliminated as they start with connectors which means they are parts of the predicate. So, options a) and c) get ruled out.

Step 2. Arranging the predicate

If we take 2 as the opening part, the sequence may be 2341, which makes complete sense. With 4 as the first part, the sequence may be 413... but including 2 gives an absurd sense. 4 cannot be followed by 3 or 2, hence, d) is eliminated.

Therefore option b) is the correct one.

Example 3.

1: environmental and psychological stress and strain

2: he said that

3: the development of positive attitudes to cope with

4: what the world needed today was

    (a) 1432   (b) 2341

    (c) 4213   (d) 2431

Step 1. Locating the subject

By observation, any of the four parts may be the subject, provided they can take a suitable predicate for themselves.

Step 2. Arranging the predicate

None of the other three fits as predicate to 1. So, option a) is eliminated.

2 as the subject may take the sequence 2431 which makes correct sense. It may take 2314 or 2134, both of which are meaningless. So, option b) is ruled out.

With either 3 or 4 as the subject, only 1 can follow it and the rest do not fit. Hence, option c) is wrong.

Therefore, option d) is correct.

II. Now, we shall discuss the jumbled paragraph, wherein the sentences of the paragraph are given in a random order and need to be sequenced logically.

THINGS TO BEAR IN MIND/ STRATEGIES TO FOLLOW:

1. Every passage will have a central theme. It helps to identify it and sequence the sentences logically in accordance with the structure of
   (i) Premise
   (ii) Support
   (iii) Example
   (iv) Progression
   (v) Conclusion
   Often, the opening sentence starts with 'it is...'
2. The opening sentence will have a noun rather than a pronoun. That is, it will introduce a person, place, body, group or any other entity.
3. Sentences bearing personal pronouns, that is, you, he, she, it, him, her, they or demonstrative pronouns this, that, these, those will always come later. They establish pairs with other noun-bearing sentence of the paragraph.
4. Adjectives showing a degree of comparison, for example better, more, worse etc., establish link with other sentences.
5. Some links or pairs of sentences of the given paragraph can be identified from the options. These may be based on the subject, time sequence (then, later, next, before, after etc.), noun-pronoun sequence, etc.
6. Sometimes, a sentence stands as an example of another. It will always come later than the sentence for which it is working as an example.
7. Signal words of <u>support</u>, for example *and, also, as well, beside, to, in fact, moreover, likewise, similarly, additionally, furthermore*, etc.;

   and of <u>contrast</u>, for example *although, yet, despite, in spite of, instead of, while, whereas, on the other hand, on the contrary, nevertheless, none the less, however, still, ironically, surprisingly, paradoxically* etc. are never the opening sentence. They follow the sentence that they support or contrast.
8. Words such as *therefore, because, consequently, hence, thus, given that, in order to, when/if...then, so/such...that, accordingly* etc. Also show pairs of cause and effect sentences, where one causes or determines another which follows it logically.
9. While the whole paragraph will have to be rearranged when TITA (type in the answer) response is required this need not be done in multiple-choice type. The best course is to eliminate options and zero in on the right one as fast as one can.

REARRANGING WORDS OR SENTENCES

EXAMPLES BASED ON LATEST PATTERN

1. If sentence (B) "The Finance Ministry's warning to potential investors in bitcoin and other cryptocurrencies has come at a time when a new, seemingly attractive investment area has opened up that few have enough information about." is the first sentence, what is the order of other sentences after rearrangement?

    (A) One of the main reasons for this volatility is speculation and the entry into the market of a large number of people lured by the prospect of quick and easy profits.

    (B) The Finance Ministry's warning to potential investors in bitcoin and other cryptocurrencies has come at a time when a new, seemingly attractive investment area has opened up that few have enough information about.

    (C) A number of investors, daunted by the high price of bitcoin, have put their money into less well-established and often spurious cryptocurrencies, only to lose it all.

    (D) Investment in bitcoin and other cryptocurrencies increased tremendously in India over the past year, but most new users know close to nothing of the technology, or how to verify the genuineness of a particular cryptocurrency.

    (E) The price of bitcoin, the most popular of all cryptocurrencies, not only shot up by well over 1000% over the course of the last year but also fluctuated wildly.

    (F) The government's caution comes on top of three warnings issued by the Reserve Bank of India since 2013.

    (a) CDEFA (b) EAFDC
    (c) DCAEF (d) ECDAF
    (e) FEDAC

2. If sentence (C) "Clinical trials involving human subjects have long been a flashpoint between bioethicists and clinical research organisations (CROs) in India." is the first sentence, what is the order of other sentences after rearrangement?

    (A) Such over-volunteering occurs more frequently in bioequivalence studies, which test the metabolism of generics in healthy subjects.

    (B) Landmark amendments to the Drugs and Cosmetics Act in 2013 led to better protection of vulnerable groups such as illiterate people, but more regulation is needed to ensure truly ethical research.

(C) Clinical trials involving human subjects have long been a flashpoint between bioethicists and clinical research organisations (CROs) in India.

(D) The big problem plaguing clinical research is an over-representation of low-income groups among trial subjects.

(E) While CROs have argued that more rules will stifle the industry, the truth is that ethical science is often better science.

(F) Sometimes CROs recruit them selectively, exploiting financial need and medical ignorance, at other times people over-volunteer for the money.

(a) ABDFE (b) BDEAF
(c) DFAEB (d) BEDFA
(e) DFABE

3. If sentence (A) "The fresh round of economic sanctions imposed unanimously by the UN Security Council on North Korea is a predictable response to mounting international frustration over the nuclear stand-off. " is the first sentence, what is the order of other sentences after rearrangement?

(A) The fresh round of economic sanctions imposed unanimously by the UN Security Council on North Korea is a predictable response to mounting international frustration over the nuclear stand-off.

(B) Despite the crippling nature of the curbs, there is some good news on this imbroglio.

(C) The measures come days after the U.S., echoing suspicions in other countries, charged the North Korean government with the world-wide 'WannaCry' cyber attacks in May.

(D) As on previous occasions, Beijing and Moscow were able to impress upon the Security Council the potentially destabilising and hence counterproductive impact of extreme measures.

(E) The sanctions include an 89% curb on refined petroleum imports into North Korea, stringent inspections of ships transferring fuel to the country, and the expulsion of thousands of North Koreans in other countries within two years.

(F) This is significant given the intercontinental ballistic missile that Pyongyang launched in November.

(a) CEBDF (b) BDCEF
(c) CFEBD (d) BEDFC
(e) DFCBE

REARRANGING WORDS OR SENTENCES

ANSWERS & EXPLANATION

1. **(b)** The first sentence talks about the fact that only few investors have idea about bitcoins and other cryptocurrencies (which seems an attractive investment area), so, the finance ministry has warned the potential investors about it. Sentence E will follow the first sentence because it says that 'bitcoin not only shot up well over by 1000%......' which justifies 'attractive investment area' and forms a link. Now, we are left with only option (b) and (d) to choose from. When we consider the sentence F, we can see that this line seems to be a part somewhere in the middle of the paragraph, also, the first line starts with a warning, therefore, it must justify the consequences of the investment in bitcoins and other cryptocurrencies which is justified by sentence C. Hence, option (b) is the correct choice.

2. **(d)** After reading all the sentences carefully, we see that sentence A and F should go one after another as both talk about 'over-volunteer'. Moreover, sentence A will follow sentence F because of the presence of the word 'such' which signifies that the subject of the sentence has already been discussed in the previous sentence. So, we have option (c), (d) and (e) to choose from. Considering sentence D which talks about 'a big problem', we find that it can't be the second sentence as no problem of any sort has been dealt in the first sentence, so, option (c) and (e) gets eliminated. Hence, by elimination method, we can conclude that option (d) is the correct choice.

3. **(a)** After reading all the sentences carefully, we see that sentence B and E should go one after another as both talk about 'curb'. Moreover, sentence B will follow sentence E because of the presence of 'the crippling nature of the curb' which signifies that the curb has already been discussed in the previous line. So, we have only option (a) and (c) to choose from. Sentence E will follow sentence C because the first line deals with 'economic sanction' making ACEB form a link. Hence, option (a) is the correct choice.

CLOZE TEST

Chapter 19: FILLING IN PARAGRAPH GAPS OR NUMBERED GAPS

A cloze test passage is a reading comprehension with some words removed. The candidate has to find the correct words from the options to fill the blanks to make the sentence grammatically as well as contextually correct. A cloze test passage has a definite structure, logical pattern and chronological order which help in maintaining a unified tone throughout.

Example 1:

_____ (1) _____ stringent anti-pollution laws, mass awareness levels in India about the need to _____ (2) _____ the environment are low. Which is _____ (3) _____ many people insist that mere laws won't do: what we _____ (4) _____ need are "environment conscious" citizens.

1. (a) Despite (b) Having
   (c) Enacting (d) Adopting
   (e) Although
2. (a) contaminate (b) clear
   (c) filter (d) protect
   (e) pollute
3. (a) resulting (b) why
   (c) obvious (d) as
   (e) because
4. (a) actually (b) don't
   (c) hardly (d) perfectly
   (e) seldom

ANSWERS & EXPLANATION

1. (a) The passage should start with a negative conjunction as the succeeding phrases states that mass awareness levels are low even though we have strict laws. Hence, option (a) is correct.

FILLING IN PARAGRAPH GAPS OR NUMBERED GAPS

2. (d) Option (e) and (a) are eliminated because after reading the sentence, it is understood that there are stringent pollution laws and even though we have laws, we couldn't secure the environment. Option (d) is correct as the sentence reads as 'need to protect the environment are low'.
3. (b) Option (b) is the correct choice. Option (a), (c) and (d) get eliminated because they are irrelevant in the context of the sentence. Between 'why' and 'because', 'because' can be eliminated as it is used as a negative conjunction. Hence, option (b) is the correct choice.
4. (a) Option (b) and (c) get eliminated as they give negative connotation when substituted in the given context. Among options (a), (d) and (e), option (a) with the word 'actually fits right into the sentence and is the best suited option. Hence, option (a) is the correct choice.

Example 2:
Reliance Infrastructure today reported 6 per cent _1_ in consolidated net profit at ₹ 382 crore for the July September quarter _2_ a dip in operating income. Total operating income declined to ₹ 5,515 crore in the quarter _3_. ₹ 5,729 crore in the same quarter _4_ fiscal, Anil Ambani led Reliance Group Company _5_ in a statement.

1. (a) extra (b) chance
   (c) rise (d) develop
   (e) waste
2. (a) admiration (b) despite
   (c) slight (d) indeed
   (e) sight
3. (a) against (b) consistent
   (c) favour (d) similar
   (e) different
4. (a) previous (b) future
   (c) following (d) further
   (e) current
5. (a) written (b) secret
   (c) said (d) thought
   (e) told

ANSWER KEY

1. (c)
2. (b)
3. (a)
4. (a)
5. (c)

NEW PATTERN BASED EXAMPLE

Example 3:

The Goods and Services Tax (GST) is being __1__ (framed) as the single-biggest economic reform since the economic liberalisation of 1991. Even critics of the tax, who complain about its complex four-slab rate structure, agree that it is a step in the right direction. The primary reason is that it __2__ (does away) with the present system of multiple Central and State taxes, replacing it with a much simpler tax system. Another supposed benefit of GST is that it is a tax on consumption, which replaces the current web of __3__ (running) taxes in the production chain that __4__ (lowers) prices and distorts production. In the process, it is said, the new tax system does away with the barriers to free trade __5__ (into) and between States, effectively turning India into a single free market for goods and services.

For __6__ (psychoanalysts), there is good reason to doubt all these claimed benefits of the GST. One, a nationwide tax such as the GST will __7__ (form) to a higher tax burden as it reduces tax competition. Earlier, States which were keen to __8__ (put in) investment and labour from each other had a reason to cut taxes. Now, the Centre, which will __9__ (increase) no tax competion except from the rest of the world, can __10__ (terminate) rates at whim. This will encourage tax rate increases that are detrimental to growth. Two, the number of taxes does not necessarily reflect the actual burden.

1. (a) turned (b) flaunted
   (c) biggest (d) oldest
   (e) No change required
2. (a) do over (b) does over
   (c) done over (d) done up
   (e) No change required
3. (a) giving (b) devastating
   (c) cascading (d) lower
   (e) No change required
4. (a) controls (b) remarket
   (c) decrease (d) increase
   (e) No change required
5. (a) in (b) on
   (c) within (d) onto
   (e) No change required

FILLING IN PARAGRAPH GAPS OR NUMBERED GAPS

6. (a) suptics (b) astrologists
    (c) people (d) predicament
    (e) No change required
7. (a) promote (b) diminish
    (c) administer (d) lead
    (e) No change required
8. (a) attract (b) commit
    (c) advice (d) adore
    (e) No change required
9. (a) arrange (b) conflict
    (c) fare (d) advocate
    (e) No change required
10. (a) determine (b) admire
    (c) desire (d) cultivate
    (e) No change required

ANSWER KEY

1. (b)
2. (e)
3. (c)
4. (d)
5. (c)
6. (a)
7. (d)
8. (a)
9. (c)
10. (a)

IMPORTANT TIPS AND TECHNIQUES

> Read the entire passage slowly and thoroughly without filling up the blanks. This will help you to understand the idea or the theme of the passage which will help you later on while choosing the options to fill the blanks.
> It is very important to understand the tone of the passage as this will help you eliminate the irrelevant options.

- Emphasize on linking the sentences together because in the passage, all the sentences are connected to each other. Do not make a mistake of treating each sentence like an individual or an independent sentence. Try to come up with logical connections that link up the sentences because this will be very helpful in picking up the correct option.
- You will often come across a blank that has more than one correct option. List out all these options and try them one by one. Use the one that seems most fitting. Instead of getting confused, think of words that are appropriate not only to the given sentence but also fit the context of the entire passage.
- Sometimes, you may not be able to decide between two words. In this case, if you see a word in the options that is frequently used with the words around the blank, then pick that option.
- The knowledge of how prepositions are used will surely come handy. There are times when looking at preposition alone can help you pick the correct option.
- It is always advised to look at the sentences that come before and after the sentence that has blank in it. By doing so, quite often you will get a confirmation or some sort of clue regarding the most appropriate word to fill.
- Read articles, especially in newspapers and magazines to improve your language. When you read more, you develop an idea of using various words in different contexts. You also get to read lot of idioms and phrases that prove to be very helpful while picking up the correct choice.

SPOTTING ERRORS

Chapter 20

SPOTTING ERRORS

Despite possessing a good command of the English language and considering ourselves well-versed in it, we many times end up making the silliest of errors in grammar. Every English exam/test contains questions on 'spotting errors' to test the grammatical knowledge of the candidate. Thus, in order to enhance your grammatical knowledge and make you aware of common errors that you usually commit while speaking and writing, we are giving very important tips and techniques to spot errors.

- Some nouns are singular in form, but they are used as plural nouns and always take a plural verb. Examples of such nouns are – Police, People, Company, Cattle and Peasantry etc.

   Sentence examples:

   Police has reached the crime spot. (**INCORRECT**)

   Police have reached the crime spot, (**CORRECT**)

   The *cattle is* grazing in the ground. (**INCORRECT**)

   The *cattle are* grazing in the ground. (**CORRECT**)

- Some nouns are always used in plural form and always take a plural verb. Examples of such nouns are – Spectacles, Scissors, Trousers, Premises and Alms etc.

   Sentence examples:

   Where *is* my trousers? (**INCORRECT**)

   Where *are* my trousers? (**CORRECT**)

   The scissors *is* on the rack. (**INCORRECT**)

   The scissors *are* on the rack. (**CORRECT**)

- There are nouns that indicate length, measure, money, weight or number and when they are preceded by a numeral, they remain unchanged in form so long as they are followed by another noun or pronoun. Examples of such nouns are – Year, Pair Foot Meter and Million etc.

Sentence examples:

This is a *ten-meters* cloth. (**INCORRECT**)

This is a *ten-meter* cloth. (**CORRECT**)

He has completed a *three-years* degree course. (**INCORRECT**)

He has completed a *three-year* degree course. (**CORRECT**)

➢ When a number is followed by a noun denoting measure, length, money, weight or number, but these are not followed by another noun or pronoun then they take the plural form.

Sentence examples:

This mat is *five yard* long. (**INCORRECT**)

This mat is *five yards* long. (**CORRECT**)

The weight of the machine was eleven *kilogram.* (**INCORRECT**)

The weight of the machine was eleven *kilograms.* (**CORRECT**)

➢ Collective nouns such as public, team, jury, committee, audience and company etc. are used both as singular as well as plural depending on the meaning. When these words indicate a unit, the verb is singular; otherwise the verb will be plural.

Sentence examples:

The *jury was* divided in this case. (**INCORRECT**)

The *jury were* divided in this case. (**CORRECT**)

➢ A pronoun must agree with its antecedent in person, number and gender.

Examples:

Every student must bring *his* identity-card.

All employees must do *their* work in the given time.

Each of the girls should carry *her* water-bottle.

➢ The pronoun 'one' must be followed by 'one's'.

Sentence example:

One must complete *his* task in time. (**INCORRECT**)

One must complete *one's* task in time. (**CORRECT**)

One should respect *his* elders. (**INCORRECT**)

One should respect *one's* elders. (**CORRECT**)

SPOTTING ERRORS

> 'One of' always takes a plural noun after it.

Sentence examples:

This is *one of* the best *moment* of my life. **(INCORRECT)**

This is *one of* the best *moments* of my life. **(CORRECT)**

One of my *friend* is an engineer. **(INCORRECT)**

One of my *friends* is an engineer. **(CORRECT)**

> Question tags are always the opposite of the sentence which means if the sentence is positive, the question tag will be negative and vice-versa.

Sentence examples:

You were quarreling, *were you?* **(INCORRECT)**

You were quarreling, *weren't you?* **(CORRECT)**

She did this, *did she?* **(INCORRECT)**

She did this, *didn't she?* **(CORRECT)**

EXAMPLES ON NEW PATTERN

The following questions consist of a sentence which is divided into three parts which contain grammatical errors in one or more than one part of the sentence. If there is an error in any part of the sentence, find the correct alternatives to replace those parts from the three options given below each question to make the sentence grammatically correct. If there is an error in any part of the sentence and none of the alternatives is correct to replace that part, then choose (d) i.e. None of the (I), (II) and (III) as your answer. If the given sentence is grammatically correct or does not require any correction, choose (e) i.e. No correction required as your answer.

1. Nearly four years after the Supreme Court recognizes the rights of transgender person,(I)/ and a few months after the approval of a policy by the State Cabinet, (II)/ the first marriage of a transgender person was registered yesterday. (III)

    (I) Nearly four years after the Supreme Court recognized the rights of transgender person,

    (II) and a few month after the approval of a policy by the State Cabinet,

    (III) the first marriage of a transgender person were registered yesterday.

    (a) Only (I) (b) Only (II)
    (c) Both (I) and (II) (d) None of the (I), (II) and (III)
    (e) No correction required

2. The government on Wednesday announced the detailed contours of the recapitalising plan for public sector banks (I)/ **it announced in October 2017,** including that a reforms package across six themes that cover 30 action points (II)/ such as customer responsiveness, responsible banking, and credit off take. (III)

   (I) The government on Wednesday announced the detailed contours of the recapitalisation plan for public sector banks
   (II) **It had announced in October 2017,** including that a reform package across six themes that cover 30 action points
   (III) such as customer responsiveness, responsible banking, and credit off take.
   (a) Only (I)   (b) Only (II)
   (c) Both (I) and (II)   (d) None of the (I), (II) and (III)
   (e) No correction required

3. The centre has decided to borrow an additional sum of money in the last three months (I)/ of this financial year, a move that some economists said could result in (II)/ the government missing its budgeted fiscal deficit target. (III)

   (I) The centre has decided to borrow additional sum of money in the last three months
   (II) of this financial year, a move that some economists said may result in
   (III) government missing its budget fiscal deficit target.
   (a) Only (II)   (b) Only (III)
   (c) Both (II) and (III)   (d) None of the (I), (II) and (III)
   (e) No correction required

4. Given the recent media reports about fresh transgressions by the Chinese troops on the Line of Actual Control (LAC) since the Doklam crisis, (I)/ it is now safe to say that the high-octane national security rhetoric by the Indian government (II)/ has done little to strengthen India's military stance at the disputed border. (III)

   (I) Given the recent media reports about fresh transgressions by the Chinese troops on the Line of Actual Control (LAC) since the Doklam crisis,
   (II) it is now safe to say that the high-octane national security rhetoric by the Indian government
   (III) has done little to strengthen India's military stance on the disputed border.
   (a) Only (I)   (b) Only (II)
   (c) Only (III)   (d) None of the (I), (II) and (III)
   (e) No correction required

SPOTTING ERRORS

5. The company will set up ten laboratories in Northern India to test, verify and calibrate (I)/ the work and reference standards of different types of balances, (II)/ weights and measuring equipments used in shops or establishments. (III)
   (I) The company will set up ten laboratories in Northern India to test, verify and calibrate
   (II) the working and reference standards of different types of balances,
   (III) weights and measuring equipments used in shops or establishments.
   (a) Only (I)   (b) Only (II)
   (c) Both (I) and (III) (d) None of the (I), (II) and (III)
   (e) No correction required

6. To the translation and interpretation of the Scriptures men might bring a fallible judgment, (I)/ but this would be assisted by (II)/ the direct action of the Spirit of God in proportion to their faith. (III)
   (I) To the translation and interpretation of the Scriptures men might bring fallible judgments,
   (II) but this will be assisted by
   (III) the direct action of the Spirit of God on proportion to their faith.
   (a) Only (I)   (b) Only (II)
   (c) Both (I) and (III) (d) None of the (I), (II) and (III)
   (e) No correction required

7. It is a true fact that in the next 5-6 years, (I)/ by when the high-speed trains would start running, (II)/ the project will more than prove itself even to its wildest of detractors. (III)
   (I) It is a fact that in the next 5-6 years,
   (II) by then the high-speed trains would start running,
   (III) the project will more than prove itself even to its wildest of detractor.
   (a) Only (I)   (b) Only (II)
   (c) Both (I) and (III) (d) None of the (I), (II) and (III)
   (e) No correction required

8. Raman was a good teacher but despite this fact, (I)/ he had no influence (II)/ on his pupils. (III)
   (I) Despite of Raman's being a good teacher,
   (II) he didn't had any influence
   (III) over his pupils
   (a) Only (I)   (b) Only (II)
   (c) Only (III)   (d) None of the (I), (II) and (III)
   (e) No correction required

9. Though the place was very scary, (I)/ he insisted to go there but we were fortunate (II)/ that we reached our home safely. (III)
   (I) In spite the place was very scary,
   (II) he insisted to going there but we were fortunate
   (III) that we reached our home safe.
   (a) Only (I)　　　　　(b) Only (II)
   (c) Both (II) and (III)　(d) None of the (I), (II) and (III)
   (e) No correction required

10. Since he was a translator, it was duck soup (I)/ for him to translate 15 pages from (II)/ Hindi to English in a single day. (III)
    (I) Him being a translator, it was duck soup
    (II) to translate 15 page from
    (III) Hindi into English in a single day.
    (a) Only (I)　　　　　(b) Only (II)
    (c) Only (III)　　　　(d) None of the (I), (II) and (III)
    (e) No correction required

ANSWERS & EXPLANATION

1. (a) Part (I) of the question is incorrect due to the use of the word 'recognizes', which should be replaced with the past tense word 'recognized' as it goes with the context of the sentence and makes the sentence grammatically correct.

2. (c) In part (I), 'recapitalising' should be replaced with 'recapitalisation' as noun should be used and not verb in the context of the sentence. In part (II), 'had' should be used before 'announced' because when we describe an action with reference to a timeframe, or an event of the past, we use past perfect tense. Part (III) is grammatically correct hence, it doesn't require any correction.

3. (e)

4. (c) Part (III) of the question is incorrect. 'on' preposition should be used instead of 'at' in the context of the sentence.

5. (b) Part (II) of the question is incorrect. 'work' which is a noun is incorrect in the context of the sentence and therefore, it should be replaced with 'working' which is an adjective to make the sentence grammatically correct.

SPOTTING ERRORS

6. (e)
7. (a) 'True' and 'fact' should not be used together as they make the sentence superfluous hence, part (I) in the question should be replaced by option (I).
8. (c) 'On' preposition should be replaced with 'over' because 'on' is incorrect in the context of the sentence whereas, 'over' makes the sentence grammatically correct.
9. (c) 'Go' which is a verb in part (II) of the sentence should be replaced with 'going' which is a noun and 'safely' which is an adverb in part (III) of the sentence should be replaced with 'safe' which is an adjective to make the sentence grammatically correct.
10. (c) 'To' preposition in part (III) of the sentence is incorrect so, it should be replaced by the preposition 'into' to make the sentence grammatically correct.

SENTENCE COMPLETION

Chapter 21

SENTENCE COMPLETION

Sentence completion is a type of test in which a word or two are removed and you are to select the most appropriate word(s) from the given options so that the sentence remains grammatically and contextually correct. This section tests your vocabulary skills and reading practice. Your abilities to understand the main idea of the sentence and the logical structure of the sentence are also tested.

Examples:

1. Because of his _____, David's father-in-law felt very welcome and comfortable staying at his house for the weekend.
   - (a) animosity
   - (b) hospitality
   - (c) determination
   - (d) wittiness
   - (e) severity

2. Although the warring partners had settled a lot of disputes, past experience made them _____ to express optimism that the talks would be a success.
   - (a) scornful
   - (b) reticent
   - (c) ambivalent
   - (d) rash
   - (e) hateful

3. It became abundantly clear that there was nothing more that could be done to save the _____ business, as years of irreversible and poor decisions had been contributing to its slow decay.
   - (a) myopic
   - (b) monumental
   - (c) mutable
   - (d) moribund
   - (e) motley

4. Because the Parliament has the votes to override a presidential veto, the President has no choice but to _____.
   - (a) object
   - (b) repel
   - (c) capitulate
   - (d) abstain
   - (e) compromise

5. Because the man had told so many _____ tales about seeing tigers, none of his friends believed him when he actually did see a tiger.
   - (a) fallacious
   - (b) verifiable
   - (c) scrupulous
   - (d) fictitious
   - (e) concrete

SENTENCE COMPLETION

6. Although some think the term 'bug' and 'insect' are _____, the former term actually refers to _____ group of insects.
   (a) parallel, an identical
   (b) precise, an exact
   (c) interchangeable, a particular
   (d) exclusive, a separate
   (e) similar, concise
7. His _____ sense of humour caused more _____ than he must have intended.
   (a) debunk, sobriety
   (b) wry, confusion
   (c) prominent, impudence
   (d) incorrigible, paucity
   (e) wise, deter
8. Psychology has slowly evolved into a/an _____ scientific discipline that now functions _____ with the same privileges and responsibility as other sciences.
   (a) independent, autonomously
   (b) unusual, alone
   (c) uncontrolled, dominantly
   (d) inactive, homogeneously
   (e) sanction solely

ANSWERS & EXPLANATION

1. (b) The sentence has positive connotation - David's father-in-law felt welcome and comfortable. In addition, the transition 'because' indicates that something that belongs to David has caused his father-in-law to feel welcome and comfortable. 'Animosity' and 'severity' have a negative connotation and 'determination' has a neutral connotation. 'Hospitality' and 'wittiness' both have positive connotations, but 'hospitality' best fits the context of the sentence. Hence, option (b) is the correct choice.
2. (b) The word 'although' sets up a contrast between what has occurred (success on some issues) and what can be expected to occur (success for the whole talks). Hence, the partners are reluctant to express optimism. 'Reticent' is synonymous to 'reluctant' hence, option (b) is the correct choice. All other options are either in contrast or irrelevant to the context of the sentence.
3. (d) To figure out what the missing word is, try to predict its definition by using keywords from the prompt. Here, the keywords are found in the noun clause "slow decay." The prompt hinges on a cause-and-effect relationship with the first clause, including the missing word, being the effect of the "irreversible and poor decisions" of the second clause. Thus, the

missing word must relate to the effect of a "slow decay." A slow decay would lead to death, so the missing word must mean dying or near death. Because moribund means dying, hence, choice (d) is correct. Other options do not fit here because they are irrelevant to the theme of the sentence hence get eliminated.

4. (e) Since the Parliament has the votes to override a presidential veto, the President is left with no other choice than to accept what the Parliament says or compromise with it in order to make the best of situation. Hence, option (e) is the correct choice. All other options are either vague or out of context of the sentence.

5. (d) The missing word must mean untrue or false, since then it would be a surprise to find him telling a story about "actually" seeing a tiger. Since fictitious means made up or unreal, choice (d) is correct. Option (a) is incorrect because fallacious means deceptive or misleading. While this could work in context for the missing word, the prompt (actually) only implies that the man's stories were imagined, not that they were intentionally deceptive. There is, thus, not enough information given in the prompt to support this choice. (b) is incorrect because verifiable means able to be confirmed. As such, this does not work in context. This word would imply that the man's usual tales were rooted in reality. (c) is incorrect because scrupulous means principled. This word would not describe either the man or his tales, as his tales are apparently not rooted in reality. (e) is incorrect because concrete means real, the exact opposite of the boy's usual tales. If the man's tales were typically authentic, his friends would be more likely to believe them.

6. (c) The word 'although' indicates that the two parts of the sentence are in contrast with each other. Although most people think about the terms 'bug' and 'insect' one way, something else is actually true about the terms. Option (c) logically completes the sentence, indicating that while most people think the terms are 'interchangeable,' the term 'bug' actually refers to 'a particular' group of insects.

7. (b) The clue word in this sentence is "caused". 'Wry' means dry or twisted humour and confusion would certainly be a potential unintended effect from this speaking style. Hopefully, you are able to use the process of elimination on many of these answer choices as the dual words double the chances you will know the meaning of at least one of the words and be able to eliminate the answer choice if it does not fit. The correct answer is the option (b).

8. (a) The sentence contains attributive interpretation of the scientific discipline of the equivalent scientific discipline of pre-modifier modified content, so space should be filled with 'independent' as autonomous is independent, therefore, the answer is option (a) whereas, all other options are incorrect.

SENTENCE COMPLETION

EXAMPLES OF THE LATEST PATTERN OF QUESTIONS

DIRECTION (1-5): In question given below there are two statements, each statement consists of two blanks. You have to choose the option which provides the correct set of words that fits both the blanks in both the statements appropriately and in the same order making them meaningful and grammatically correct.

1. (A) Consumers in India are already beginning to feel the _____ as petrol and diesel prices have _____ multi-year highs.
   (B) It was her hard _____ that saved his life as he was about to get _____ by the fast moving truck.
   (a) tweak, grown   (b) pinch, hit
   (c) squeeze, knocked   (d) burden, buffeted
   (e) cramp, bumped

2. (A) The _____ of actors at the _____ concert was nothing new.
   (B) At the _____, the thieves made their _____ plan to execute in the very next day.
   (a) get-together, plummet
   (b) meeting, grisly
   (c) tryst, appalling
   (d) amour, grotesque
   (e) rendezvous, nocturnal

3. (A) His tough _____ with the dealer made sure that he was very concerned about the proper _____ of his family in the new city.
   (B) In the current state of Brexit _____, a spirit of reasonable _____ could well define the future.
   (a) dealings, settlement
   (b) arguments, compliance
   (c) negotiations, accommodation
   (d) talks, conniption
   (e) dispute, leniency

4. (A) The _____, which are generally conducted between January and March, had a late start this year, and were less _____ than were seen in recent years.
   (B) The military _____ administered by the Indian army showed _____ use of indigenously built fighter jets.
   (a) manoeuvre, extensive
   (b) tactic, stunning
   (c) exercise, capacious
   (d) activity, amorphous
   (e) cessation, huge

SENTENCE COMPLETION

5. (A) His love for cars never _____ because even in his old age, he used to _____ short his spending to buy the latest one in the market.
   (B) Indian gold demand _____ as jewellers expected import tax _____ in budget.
   (a) diminished, slit
   (b) dwindled, rip
   (c) waned, cut
   (d) drooped, chip
   (e) decreased, praise

ANSWER KEY

11. (b)
12. (e)
13. (c)
14. (a)
15. (c)

IMPORTANT TIPS AND TECHNIQUES TO SOLVE SENTENCE COMPLETION

➢ It is advised not to look at the options straightaway. At first, read the sentence and think of a word that fits in the blank appropriately. This strategy will help you find the missing word easily because when you read the sentence, you catch the theme, tone and context of the sentence.

➢ When you look at the options, make sure you find the option that best replaces the word that you had thought of initially. Ensure that the meaning of the sentence is intact. Once you have placed the likely option, do check that the sentence gives out a plausible meaning.

➢ Concentrate on eliminating the options rather than finding the correct one. In sentence completion test, your knowledge and understanding of vocabulary and common idioms-phrases of English language is tested. You must consider all of the choices before you confirm your answer, even if your predicted answer is among the choices. The difference between the best answer and the second best answer is sometimes very subtle. When you think that you have the correct answer, read the entire sentence to yourself, using your best choice.

➢ Keeping a close eye on grammar rules can sometimes help you find the correct word easily. For instance, if the article 'an' comes before the blank then you can immediately go for the option that begins with a vowel or a word the pronunciation of which sounds like a vowel.

SENTENCE COMPLETION

- You should look for indicators in the sentence; if any. Indicators tell you what is coming up. They indicate that the part of the sentence is either drawing a contrast with something stated previously or supporting something stated previously. Examples of some contrast indicators are – But, Despite, Although, However, Nevertheless and Yet etc. Examples of some support indicators are – And, For, Likewise, Also, Furthermore, Moreover and In addition, etc. Examples of cause and effect indicators are – Thus, Therefore, Hence, Because, If...then, etc.

- Lastly, read English newspapers and magazines regularly as this will enhance your grammatical understanding and you will also come to see how various words are used in different contexts. Reading habits, at times, help you get the correct word just by having a quick glance at the options.

Chapter 22

PASSAGE COMPLETION

Passage completion is a test in which a paragraph is given with an omitted line and you have to find this omitted line from the given options.

For example:

1. Women's boxing is yet to be recognized as an Olympic support, _____. If that happens, the dream of most of the tough girls may come true.
   (A) The International Boxing Association has been campaigning to include it as an event in the 2008 Beijing Olympics.
   (B) Though boxing is a very tough sport many women are seen willing to take up professional boxing now-a-days.
   (C) Even some state governments are now willing to employ the women pugilists.
   (a) Only A (b) Only B
   (c) Both A and C (d) Both B and C
   (e) All A, B and C

2. Although the share of agriculture in the overall GDP has declined from around 40 per cent in 1980-81 to below 20 per cent in 2006-07, its importance to the Indian economy can hardly be over-emphasized. _____. In the context of ensuring food security and promoting inclusive growth, strategies to revitalize agriculture has become highly relevant.
   (A) Fiscal deficits as a proportion of the GDP have come down but are still high by global standards.
   (B) Infrastructure deficiencies can hold back further grown in the agriculture sector.
   (C) Recent Volatility in agricultural production has had its impact not only on economic but on price stability as well.
   (a) Only A (b) Only B
   (c) Only C (d) Both B and C
   (e) None of these

3. The audiences for crosswords and Sudoku, understandably, overlap greatly, but there are differences, too. A crossword attracts a more literary person, while Sudoku appeals to a keenly logical mind. Some crossword enthusiasts turn up their noses at Sudoku because they feel it lacks depth. A good crossword requires vocabulary, knowledge, mental flexibility and sometimes even a sense of humour to complete. It touches numerous areas of life and provides an 'Aha!' or two along the way. _____

PASSAGE COMPLETION

(a) Sudoku, on the other hand, is just a logical exercise, each one similar to the last.
(b) Sudoku, incidentally, is growing faster in popularity than crosswords, even among the literati.
(c) Sudoku, on the other hand, can be attempted and enjoyed even by children.
(d) Sudoku, however, is not exciting in any sense of the term.
(e) Sudoku, whereas, gives better enthusiasm.

4. Mental illness is often stigmatized. _____ It is not as obviously fatal as many physical illnesses. But it still takes a heavy human and economic toll. That is why, it is important that politicians make good on their promises and that ordinary people dig deep, too.

(a) Though the brain is extraordinarily complex, further scientific breakthroughs can be expected.
(b) Post-traumatic stress disorder was only defined in 1980; understanding of that condition has jumped forward in the past few years, as have the treatments for it.
(c) Past investigations into early interventions in psychosis have since repaid themselves many times over.
(d) Many illnesses afflict the old disproportionately, but mental illness tends to strike the young, undermining productivity.
(e) It lacks an effective lobby to match the groups that represent victims of cancer and heart disease.

ANSWERS & EXPLANATION

1. (a) The first sentence says that women's boxing has not been recognized as an Olympic sport. Sentence A follows with the idea that the Indian Boxing Association is campaigning towards it being included in the 2008 Olympics. Taking up boxing as a profession or getting a government job as mentioned in sentences B and C cannot be a great 'dream' to be fulfilled which is the idea stated in the last sentence.

2. (c) The opening sentence highlights the importance of agriculture in the Indian economy. Sentence C follows emphasizing the fact that volatility in agriculture production can have various undesirable impacts. Hence, we have to revitalize agricultural field and this is the idea given in the last sentence. The other two sentences talk about 'fiscal deficits' and infrastructure deficiencies in the agricultural sector which are irrelevant in the given context.

3. (a) The paragraph, in the beginning, highlights the main points of difference between Sudoku and a crossword. Therefore, we are looking for a contrast, which is not present in options (b) and (d). Option (c) is too specific, which is why we pick Option (a).

4. (e) In the next statement after the blank, mental illness is compared with physical illness and is said that politicians and people should take this matter seriously. Now in option (e) also, mental illness is compared with cancer and heart disease that are physical illness and it is said that it lacks effective lobby to match.

TIPS AND TECHNIQUES TO SOLVE PASSAGE COMPLETION

- ➤ It is very important to read the passage without missing any line to understand the inherent message/view/opinion the author wants to convey. This also helps you out in drawing the topic or the central idea of the passage which is vital while choosing the correct option.
- ➤ After reading the passage carefully, have a glance on the options and try to find the correct sentence by matching the subject-matter/topic of the passage with that of the given options.
- ➤ The options which appear to be irrelevant or out of context should be ignored instantly.
- ➤ After eliminating the mismatch options, you will be left with two or may be three options to choose from. Now, you need to judge which of the left options matches with the tone of the author and correctly fits the blank.
- ➤ Try to find the selected options one by one at the missing space and judge it on the basis of tone, context, logic, sequence and symmetry. The option which qualifies these criteria will be the right one and should be chosen.
- ➤ After finding the correct option, read the passage for the last time to finally conclude that after filling the blank with your selected option, the passage reflects a complete picture/ meaning.

Chapter 23 REVISION EXERCISES

CLOZE TEST

DIRECTIONS (Qs. 1-10) : In the passage given below, there are 10 blanks, each followed by a word given in bold. Every blank has four alternative words given in options (a),(b),(c) and (d). You have to tell which word will best suit the respective blank. Mark (e) as your answer if the word given in bold after the blank is your answer i.e "No change required".

Everyone knows that the baby-boomer generation is in the process of retiring, and that all those ex-hippies and _1_(impish) can expect to live longer than the Americans who retired before them. But the financial challenge this poses is less well understood. Any lingering _2_(anxiety) ought to be exploded by two papers in the latest *Journal of Retirement*.

The first*, from the Centre for Retirement Research (CRR) at Boston College, estimates the proportion of 65-year-olds who will be able to retire without a big hit to their _3_(boorish) income. Pensioners do not usually need as much money coming in as workers: for a start, they no longer need to save for retirement. The CRR estimates that 65-85% of their previous income is a reasonable "replacement rate", depending on the type of household.

As well as private pensions, elderly Americans receive income from the federal government (in the form of Social Security, the public pension) and many earn money from their accumulated wealth, particularly by taking _4_(equity) out of their houses. Even allowing for these sources of income, the CRR estimates that 52% of Americans may not be able to maintain their standard of living (which it defines as having an income that falls no more than 10% below the replacement rate).

Unsurprisingly, the biggest problems face those with no private pension at all: 68% of these Americans are expected to fall short. Those lucky enough to be covered by defined-benefit plans—in which pensions are linked to a worker's salary—have the least difficulty: only 20% are _5_(risk) at risk. Of those in defined-contribution (DC) plans—in which workers receive whatever pension _6_(deduced) they have accumulated by retirement—53% probably will not reach the replacement rate.

At least, you might think, Social Security will provide a basic income for the elderly. But the second paper**, by Sylvester Schieber, a former chairman of the Social Security Advisory Board, _7_(dramatized) that there are holes in the safety net. Mr Schieber finds that people whose total careers _8_(fronted) just 10-

19 years comprise 8% of pensioners, but just over half of the poorest tenth of the elderly. Such workers could hardly have saved more for their retirement; they had barely _9_ (intolerable) income in the first place.

That could be a _10_ (languid) problem, given Social Security's finances. Payroll taxes on current workers no longer exceed the benefits paid out, prompting the government to tap the surplus of past years. On current projections, this will run out in 2034. After that, the cost of pensions could still be met mainly by contributions from workers. But the politicians of the day may be forced to consider benefit cuts.

1. (a) brats (b) punks
   (c) bleats (d) bonnets
   (e) No Change Required
2. (a) modest (b) burden
   (c) altruism (d) complacency
   (e) No Change Required
3. (a) turbid (b) essential
   (c) disposable (d) enhance
   (e) No Change Required
4. (a) partial (b) empathy
   (c) liquidity (d) dispense
   (e) No Change Required
5. (a) deemed (b) doubted
   (c) regarded (d) nundated
   (e) No Change Required
6. (a) box (b) pot
   (c) dribble (d) dethrone
   (e) No Change Required
7. (a) kindled (b) evoke
   (c) draw out (d) points out
   (e) No Change Required
8. (a) perished (b) arched
   (c) strived (d) lasted
   (e) No Change Required
9. (a) shy (b) skimpy
   (c) adequate (d) waiting
   (e) No Change Required
10. (a) isolating (b) looming
    (c) receding (d) holding
    (e) No Change Required

REVISION EXERCISES

DIRECTIONS (Qs. 11-15) : In the following passage, some of the words have been left out, each of which is indicated by a number. Find the suitable word from the options given against each number and fill up the blanks with appropriate words to make the paragraph meaningfully complete.

Land problems in India continue to attract equal attention from policy-makers and academics. The renewed interest in land issues _11_ from the _12_ impact of liberalisation and _13_ the economy. Tenancy, land ceiling and land administration are being _14_ with a new perspective. Among the issues under renewed focus, legalizing tenancy, revising the ceiling limits, quality of land, meeting the challenge of miniscule holdings that are _15_ of marginalisation and land administration are dominating the debate.

11. (a) clears (b) finds
    (c) tools (d) stems
    (e) fires
12. (a) commenced (b) perceived
    (c) migrated (d) less
    (e) pioneer
13. (a) agitate (b) materialize
    (c) opening up (d) suffer
    (e) slope
14. (a) revisited (b) renowned
    (c) used (d) termed
    (e) havocked
15. (a) start (b) lcvel
    (c) status (d) inception
    (e) consequences

DIRECTIONS (Qs. 16-20) : In the following passage, some of the words have been left out, each of which is indicated by a number. Find the suitable word from the options given against each number and fill up the blanks with appropriate words to make the paragraph meaningfully complete.

A good percentage of the population of India is tribal. They live in the hills and forests of the country; and have been little........(16)........ by the .... (17)........ currents of the plains. Practically all the states of India have their tribal population. The tribes are numerous, computed to be about 200, some living in........(18)........regions in dense forests, and others on the borders of villages. Some tribes are ....(19)........to a few souls, while others like the Santhals run into millions and are steadily........(20)........in numbers.

16. (a) affected (b) domiciled
    (c) motivated (d) deprived
    (e) favoured

17. (a) financial (b) proud
    (c) cultural (d) unruly
    (e) swift
18. (a) comfortable (b) marshy
    (c) wild (d) unpopulated
    (e) inhospitable
19. (a) devoted (b) confined
    (c) susceptible (d) related
    (e) attached
20. (a) constant (b) deteriorated
    (c) developing (d) increasing
    (e) decreasing

DOUBLE FILLERS

DIRECTIONS (Qs. 21-35) : In question given below there are two statements, each statement consists of two blanks. You have to choose the option which provides the correct set of words that fits both the blanks in both the statements appropriately and in the same order making them meaningful and grammatically correct.

21. (1) With a firm _____, the government should be able to focus more on the strategy to further _____ growth and demand.
    (2) They can't accept the attack on their electoral _____ which has the chances to negatively _____ their voters.
    (a) edict, deter (b) mandate, stimulate
    (c) directives, appease (d) denial, prompt
    (e) authority, dissuade

22. (1) It is a great misfortune that an internal _____ has moved _____ towards a full-blow crisis.
    (2) While _____ still exists between the status of men and women in the world, the tide of history is flowing _____ in favour of women.
    (a) controversy, wrongly (b) unity, adamantly
    (c) cleft, impeccably (d) concordance, doggedly
    (e) rift, inexorably

23. (1) He appeared to be the _____ as everyone in the party was _____ about him.
    (2) Being the _____ of the meeting, he was busy _____ about the new project laid by his company.
    (a) cynosure, talking (b) nonentity, discussing
    (c) hotshot, sceptical (d) linchpin, aporetic
    (e) boss, incredulous

REVISION EXERCISES
145

24. (1) As the sun rose higher in the sky, the temperature _____ into hundreds and Martha felt her energy begin to _____.
    (2) The _____ prices of onion in the last month resulted in _____ its consumption.
    (a) increased, improve (b) drifted, lessen
    (c) ascended, enhance (d) soared, dwindle
    (e) towered, increase

25. (1) The soldier refused to accept a _____ for his bravery because he felt he was _____ performing his duty.
    (2) The inexperienced singer was surprised to receive a _____ for _____ singing in the chorus.
    (a) compliment, ambiguously
    (b) reward, effortlessly
    (c) plaudit, simply
    (d) bestowal, normally
    (e) citation, callously

26. (1) In order to _____ himself from the beating of his father, the student thought to _____ a way to cheat in the examination.
    (2) To _____ their businesses, the black marketers have _____ with the police in a shoddy business.
    (a) protect, cogitate (b) secure, confederate
    (c) save, connive (d) bulwark, plot
    (e) defend, scheme

27. (1) His _____ towards his brother led him to _____ his car.
    (2) Since I bear no _____ towards you, I don't understand what provoked you to _____ the boundary of my campus.
    (a) animosity, eradicate (b) grudge, repair
    (c) antipathy, devastate (d) malice, vandalize
    (e) benevolence, build

28. (1) The dollar has been gradually _____ against major currencies _____ the beginning of the last year.
    (2) The increasing difference between the rich and poor has resulted in _____ of people's faith in our democracy _____ independence.
    (a) depreciating, since (b) growing, from
    (c) undermining, from (d) crippling, since
    (e) weakening, since

29. (1) Monika used to walk _____ foot for five kilometers to look after her father who was _____ in the city hospital.
    (2) The chief minister in the party meeting stressed _____ the view shared by one of his ministers as two days ago, he in a press conference _____ that the state government was not doing its work up to the mark.
    (a) on, accepted (b) over, abstained
    (c) on, admitted (d) over, put
    (e) at, repudiated

REVISION EXERCISES

30. (1) The increasing burden of loans on the company has forced it to _____ from _____ to CSR.
    (2) As rising oil prices put pressure on domestic consumers, the government will have to _____ from _____ to subsidies.
    (a) desist, resorting   (b) cease, addressing
    (c) relinquish, dodging   (d) endure, procuring
    (e) recover, providing

31. (1) A _____ driver was arrested yesterday on a drunk driving _____ on the Delhi-Chandigarh Highway.
    (2) An erstwhile _____ department in the ministry of commerce, the Department of Industrial Policy and Promotion (DIPP), was put in _____ of this transformation.
    (a) inactive, headlong   (b) lazy, impeach
    (c) headstrong, arraign   (d) sleepy, charge
    (e) slumber, contact

32. (1) Economic growth, which had been _____ down for some time but had been given a boost by strong governance reforms was given a demand boost to facilitate _____ acceleration.
    (2) Forced _____ is when political parties hire PR agencies which _____ employ social media 'influencers' who release the same tweets with the hashtag at a high intensity.
    (a) hover, advance   (b) trending, further
    (c) going, reduce   (d) trading, more
    (e) shot, progress

33. (1) _____ remains below targets for many Central Bank; and is generally set to stay that way in the year ahead even though the world economy in general is set to do much _____ in 2018.
    (2) India did not have _____ targeting then and so was able to deal with the shocks _____ than many countries.
    (a) consumed, more   (b) inflation, better
    (c) deflation, good   (d) prices, honed
    (e) reduced, enhanced

34. (1) U.S. consumer confidence jumped to a near 17-year high in October, with households _____ about the labor market and business _____, which could underpin consumer spending and boost the economy.
    (2) The services sector was the most _____ about business prospects in over three years with about 9 per cent of firms expecting more favourable business _____ in the October to March period.
    (a) upbeat, conditions   (b) regular, placid
    (c) optimism, excellent   (d) downtrodden, environment
    (e) vulnerable, situation

REVISION EXERCISES

35. (1) We expect crude oil to _____ to USD 65 per barrel along with commodities standing their _____ against the temporary headwinds.
    (2) Should quarterly growth _____ and BJP make gains in serial state elections it would salvage lost _____ indicating a positive shift in perceptions.
    (a) increase, floor   (b) depressed, topsy
    (c) rebound, ground   (d) decline, space
    (e) slip, grip

DIRECTIONS (Qs. 36-40) : In each of the following sentences there are blank spaces. Below each sentence there are five pairs of words denoted by the numbers. Find out which pair of words can be filled up in the blanks in the sentence in the same sequence to make it grammatically correct.

36. While the technology and state of knowledge in medicine allows the gadgets to _____ data and give recommendation, it will be a while before we are ready to _____ doctors for serious illnesses.
    (a) analyse, trust   (b) evaluate, credence
    (c) figure out, confidence (d) describe, distrust
    (e) estimate, credit

37. Just because momentum is _____ away coal in china does not mean that the country is no longer part of the global coal _____.
    (a) altering, bang   (b) changing, collapse
    (c) stagnation, rise   (d) shifting, boom
    (e) staying, failure

38. There's plenty of _____ that transferring kids to the adult criminal justice system for trial and conviction has _____ to prevent repeat offences.
    (a) disproof, developed (b) indication, finished
    (c) information, rise   (d) evidence, failed
    (e) data, declined

39. However, 'Digital India' will not happen even if the _____ is in place unless equal _____ is paid to what is made available at the end of the pipeline.
    (a) framework, thinking (b) groundwork, scrutiny
    (c) infrastructure, attention (d) backbone, indifference
    (e) support, thought

40. The national disaster management authority should come up with national guidelines for the _____ of such deaths for immediate _____ by the states.
    (a) prevention, implementation
    (b) aid, effect
    (c) deterrence, operation
    (d) avoidance, usage
    (e) obstruction, assistance

SPOTTING ERRORS

DIRECTIONS (Qs. 41-60) : The following question consists of a sentence which is divided into three parts which contain grammatical errors in one or more than one part of the sentence. If there is an error in any part of the sentence, find the correct alternatives to replace those parts from the three options given below each question to make the sentence grammatically correct. If there is an error in any part of the sentence and none of the alternatives is correct to replace that part, then choose (d) i.e. None of the (I), (II) and (III) as your answer. If the given sentence is grammatically correct or does not require any correction, choose (e) i.e. No correction required as your answer.

41. Concern is rising across the security establishment over the worsening situation (I)/ along the Indo-Pakistan border, where casualties from (II)/ cross-border firing have now climbed beyond all recent trends. (III)
    (I) Concern is arising across the security establishment over the worsening situation
    (II) in the Indo-Pakistan border, where casualties from
    (III) cross-border firing has now climbed beyond all recent trends
    (a) Only (I) (b) Only (II)
    (c) Both (I) and (III) (d) None of the (I), (II) and (III)
    (e) No correction required

42. The center had issued a statement on a mutual decision for Indian and Chinese troop (I)/ to disengage and withdraw from the part of the Doklam plateau (II)/ disputed between China and Bhutan that has been the scene of the stand-off. (III)
    (I) The center had issued a statement on a mutual decision for Indian and Chinese troops
    (II) to disengage and withdraw the part of the Doklam plateau
    (III) disputed between China and Bhutan that had been the scene of the stand-off
    (a) Only (I) (b) Only (II)
    (c) Both (I) and (III) (d) None of these
    (e) No correction required

43. The quality of education could be enhanced (I)/ by granting flexibility to States, making teachers accounting, and adopting (II)/ blended learning approaches and computer-aided learning. (III)
    (I) The quality of education could enhance
    (II) by granting flexibility to States, making teachers accountable, and adopting
    (III) blended learning access and computer-aided learning
    (a) Only (I) (b) Only (II)
    (c) Both (I) and (III) (d) None of the (I), (II) and (III)
    (e) No correction required

REVISION EXERCISES

44. The writer believes that the work experience should focus more on the development (I)/ in students of the ability to work with the materials of their environment (II)/ and solve problems as close to reality as is practicable. (III)
 (I) The writer believes that the work experience should focus more in the development
 (II) in students of the ability to work with the materials of his environment
 (III) and solve problems too close to reality as is practicable
 (a) Only (I)   (b) Only (II)
 (c) Both (I) and (II)   (d) None of the (I), (II) and (III)
 (e) No correction required

45. If you had waited for me, (I)/ I would have (II)/ gone to the party too. (III)
 (I) If you have waited for me
 (II) I would have had
 (III) gone to the party also
 (a) Only (I)   (b) Only (II)
 (c) Both (I) and (III)   (d) None of the (I), (II) and (III)
 (e) No correction required

46. Nearly four years after the Supreme Court recognizes the rights of transgender person,(I)/ and a few months after the approval of a policy by the State Cabinet, (II)/ the first marriage of a transgender person was registered yesterday. (III)
 (I) Nearly four years after the Supreme Court recognized the rights of transgender person,
 (II) and a few month after the approval of a policy by the State Cabinet,
 (III) the first marriage of a transgender person were registered yesterday.
 (a) Only (I)   (b) Only (II)
 (c) Both (I) and (II)   (d) None of the (I), (II) and (III)
 (e) No correction required

47. The government on Wednesday announced the detailed contours of the recapitalising plan for public sector banks (I)/ it announced in October 2017, including that a reforms package across six themes that cover 30 action points (II)/ such as customer responsiveness, responsible banking, and credit off take. (III)
 (I) The government on Wednesday announced the detailed contours of the recapitalisation plan for public sector banks
 (II) it had announced in October 2017, including that a reforms package across six themes that cover 30 action points
 (III) such as customer responsiveness, responsible banking, and credit off take.
 (a) Only (I)   (b) Only (II)
 (c) Both (I) and (II)   (d) None of the (I), (II) and (III)
 (e) No correction required

48. The centre has decided to borrow an additional sum of money in the last three months (I)/ of this financial year, a move that some economists said could result in (II)/ the government missing its budgeted fiscal deficit target. (III)

(I) The centre has decided to borrow additional sum of money in the last three months
(II) of this financial year, a move that some economists said may result in
(III) government missing its budget fiscal deficit target.
(a) Only (II) (b) Only (III)
(c) Both (II) and (III) (d) None of the (I), (II) and (III)
(e) No correction required

49. Given the recent media reports about fresh transgressions by the Chinese troops on the Line of Actual Control (LAC) since the Doklam crisis, (I)/ it is now safe to say that the high-octane national security rhetoric by the Indian government (II)/ has done little to strengthen India's military stance at the disputed border. (III)

(I) Given the recent media reports about fresh transgressions by the Chinese troops on the Line of Actual Control (LAC) since the Doklam crisis,
(II) it is now safe to say that the high-octane national security rhetoric by the Indian government
(III) has done little to strengthen India's military stance on the disputed border.
(a) Only (I) (b) Only (II)
(c) Only (III) (d) None of the (I), (II) and (III)
(e) No correction required

50. The company will set up ten laboratories in Northern India to test, verify and calibrate (I)/ the work and reference standards of different types of balances, (II)/ weights and measuring equipments used in shops or establishments. (III)

(I) The company will set up ten laboratories in Northern India to test, verify and calibrate
(II) the working and reference standards of different types of balances,
(III) weights and measuring equipments used in shops or establishments.
(a) Only (I) (b) Only (II)
(c) Both (I) and (III) (d) None of the (I), (II) and (III)
(e) No correction required

51. To the translation and interpretation of the Scriptures men might bring a fallible judgment, (I)/ but this would be assisted by (II)/ the direct action of the Spirit of God in proportion to their faith. (III)

(I) To the translation and interpretation of the Scriptures men might bring fallible judgments,
(II) but this will be assisted by
(III) the direct action of the Spirit of God on proportion to their faith.
(a) Only (I) (b) Only (II)
(c) Both (I) and (III) (d) None of the (I), (II) and (III)
(e) No correction required

REVISION EXERCISES

52. It is a true fact that in the next 5-6 years, (I)/ by when the high-speed trains would start running, (II)/ the project will more than prove itself even to its wildest of detractors. (III)
    (I) It is a fact that in the next 5-6 years,
    (II) by then the high-speed trains would start running,
    (III) the project will more than prove itself even to its wildest of detractor.
    (a) Only (I) (b) Only (II)
    (c) Both (I) and (III) (d) None of the (I), (II) and (III)
    (e) No correction required

53. Raman was a good teacher but despite this fact, (I)/ he had no influence (II)/ on his pupils. (III)
    (I) Despite of Raman's being a good teacher,
    (II) he didn't had any influence
    (III) over his pupils..
    (a) Only (I) (b) Only (II)
    (c) Only (III) (d) None of the (I), (II) and (III)
    (e) No correction required

54. Though the place was very scary, (I)/ he insisted to go there but we were fortunate (II)/ that we reached our home safely. (III)
    (I) In spite the place was very scary,
    (II) he insisted to going there but we were fortunate
    (III) that we reached our home safe.
    (a) Only (I) (b) Only (II)
    (c) Both (II) and (III) (d) None of the (I), (II) and (III)
    (e) No correction required

55. Since he was a translator, it was duck soup (I)/ for him to translate 15 pages from (II)/ Hindi to English in a single day. (III)
    (I) Him being a translator, it was duck soup
    (II) to translate 15 page from
    (III) Hindi into English in a single day.
    (a) Only (I) (b) Only (II)
    (c) Only (III) (d) None of the (I), (II) and (III)
    (e) No correction required

56. NHRC notice, terming the case (I)/a serious violation of the right of life of patients (II)/came even as 41 more children died of since Saturday. (III)
    (I) NHRC noticed, terming the case
    (II) a seriously violation of the right to life of patients
    (III) came even as 41 more children died from Saturday.
    (a) Only (I) (b) Both (I) and (II)
    (c) All (I), (II) and (III) (d) None of (I), (II) and (III)
    (e) No correction required

57. Heavy rain in the last three days triggered flash floods (I)/ in parts of Bihar, and inundated large areas in Assam and North Bengal (II)/ paralysed normal life and snapping rail link to the North-East from the rest of the country.(III)

(I) Heavy rain in last three days triggered flash floods
(II) in parts of Bihar and inundated larger area in Assam and North Bengal
(III) paralysing normal life and snapping rail link to the North-East from the rest of the country.

(a) Only (I) (b) Only (III)
(c) Both (II) and (III) (d) All (I), (II) and (III)
(e) No correction required

58. The effects of the crisis are not just (I) / seen in the dry economic data, (II) / they are felt as well as in the gut. (III)

(I) The effects of crisis have not just
(II) seen in the dried economic data,
(III) they are felt in the gut as well.

(a) Both (I) and (II) (b) Both (II) and (III)
(c) Only (III) (d) All (I), (II) and (III)
(e) No correction required

59. The country's post-war Constitution stipulates that (I)/the emperor is no god-king above the law (II)/as he was before the country's defeat in 1945. (III)

(I) The country's post-war Constitution has been stipulated that
(II) the emperor is no god like over the law
(III) as it was before the country's defeat in 1945.

(a) Only (I) (b) Both (I) and (II)
(c) Both (II) and (III) (d) None of the (I), (II) and (III)
(e) No correction required

60. It proved to be a blunder mistake (I)/ by the Indian team to choose for (II)/ bowling after winning the toss. (III)

(I) It proved to be a blunder
(II) by the Indian team to choosing for
(III) bowling after win the toss.

(a) Only (I) (b) Both (I) and (II)
(c) Both (II) and (III) (d) None of the (I), (II) and (III)
(e) No correction required

REVISION EXERCISES

DIRECTIONS (61-80) : Which of the phrases (a), (b), (c) and (d) given below each question should replace the phrase printed in bold type to make the sentence grammatically correct? If the sentence is correct as it is given and no correction is required, mark (e) as the answer.

61. We have hired an advertising agency to prepare a campaign to encourage **people votes**.
    (a) people from voting
    (b) voting for people
    (c) people to vote
    (d) people for voting
    (e) No correction required

62. During the training program, the new recruits will be briefed **about how their role** in the new company.
    (a) what their roles
    (b) about their roles
    (c) for its roles
    (d) which are their role
    (e) No correction required

63. The machine is in such poor condition that we have **no alternative** to buy new one.
    (a) many alternative like
    (b) any alternative except
    (c) no other alternative
    (d) no alternative but
    (e) No correction required

64. Since the deadline has been changed from next week to this Monday, you should **give this work priority**.
    (a) be given this work priority
    (b) prioritized this work
    (c) priority this work
    (d) not give priority this work
    (e) No correction required

65. After the success of our project, we have been receiving **more requests than** we do not have the resources to handle them.
    (a) most of the requests
    (b) too many requests
    (c) many requests but
    (d) much requests than
    (e) No correction required

66. The Eunuchs Act, enacted in the Nizam's dominions, has been in force since 1919 explicitly to control "eunuchs", that is, people **who are both** "males in female dress" and those who had undergone "emasculation".
    (a) who were both
    (b) who are either
    (c) who were either
    (d) who use to ne
    (e) No correction required

67. Section 5 provides for the punishment of a eunuch with imprisonment if **it could be found that** he "has with him or in his house under his control" a boy who is less than 16 years old.
    (a) it has to be found
    (b) it found to be that
    (c) it's been found that
    (d) it is found that
    (e) No correction required

68. The purpose of elevating certain rights to the stature of guaranteed fundamental rights is to insulate their exercise **to disdain the** majorities, whether legislative or popular."
    (a) for disdaining of
    (b) for the disdaining of
    (c) from the disdain of
    (d) the disdain of
    (e) No correction required

69. Sexual orientation is an essential component of identity. Equal protection demands protection **the identification of** every individual without discrimination.
    (a) the identity of
    (b) for the identification of
    (c) of the identity of
    (d) as the identification of
    (e) No correction required

70. There is widespread evidence that the existence of the Eunuchs Act **which resulted** in a pervasive and continuing practice of criminalization, illegal detention, torture in custody, and extreme coercion, which includes a perennial threat of arrest.
    (a) resulted
    (b) had resulted
    (c) have resulted
    (d) has resulted
    (e) No correction required

71. The police were **barking on the wrong tree**.
    (a) barking upon the wrong tree
    (b) barking up the wrong tree
    (c) baring along the wrong tree
    (d) barking over the wrong tree
    (e) No correction required

72. Last year, a military **plane carrying** five army personnel crashed after taking off from its base camp.
    (a) plane that has carried
    (b) plane that had carried
    (c) plane was carrying
    (d) plane carried
    (e) No correction required

73. Special commandos **were rushed out from** Udhampur to Jammu for the final assault.
    (a) was rushed over
    (b) was being rushed in from
    (c) had been rushed away from
    (d) were rushed in from
    (e) No correction required

74. I am **looking forward to meeting** her in the next weekends.
    (a) looking forward to meet
    (b) looking forward upon meeting
    (c) looking forward for meeting
    (d) looking forward into meeting
    (e) No correction required

REVISION EXERCISES

75. The population of Tokyo is **greater than all other** town in the words.
    (a) greater than that of any other
    (b) greatest among any other
    (c) greater than those of any other
    (d) greater than any other
    (e) No correction required
76. The performance of our team was rather **worst that I had expected**.
    (a) bad as I had expected (b) worse than I had expected
    (c) worst than was expected (d) worse than expectation
    (e) No correction required
77. The intruder stood quietly **for few moments**.
    (a) for few time   (b) for the few moments
    (c) for moments   (d) for a few moments
    (e) No correction required
78. The policy has **so far succeeded in recovering** only a part of the stolen property.
    (a) thus far succeeded for recovery
    (b) so far succeeded in recovery of
    (c) as for as succeeded in recovery of
    (d) so far succeeded to recover
    (e) No correction required
79. He asked the crowd if they thought he was right and the crowd shouted **that he did**.
    (a) that they did   (b) that they had
    (c) that he is   (d) that he didn't
    (e) No correction required
80. Joseph, unnecessarily **picked up** a quarrel with Manu and left the party.
    (a) has picked up   (b) picked on
    (c) picked   (d) picking up
    (e) No correction required

READING COMPREHENSION

DIRECTIONS (Qs. 81-90) : Read the following passage carefully and answer the questions that follow.

Two principles are involved in the controversy about the presence of foreign controlled media in the country; the free flow of ideas and images across national borders and the need to safeguard the national interest and preserve cultural autonomy. Both are valid but both are at loggerheads because each has been used to promote less lofty goals.

The first principle conforms to a moral imperative: freedom to expression cannot rhyme with restrictions imposed by any government. But the free flow rhetoric also clouds the fact that the powerful Western, and especially American media, can and often do present, subtly or brazenly, news in a manner that promotes Western political, ideological and strategic interests. Besides, Western entertainment programs present lifestyles and values that run counter to the lifestyles and values cherished by traditional societies. All this explains why so many Indian newspapers, magazines and news agencies have sought protection from the courts to prevent foreign publications and news agencies from operating in the country. Their arguments are weak on two counts. As the bitter debate on a new world information and communication order demonstrated in the late seventies and early eighties, many of those who resent Western 'invasion' in the fields of information and culture are no great friends of democracy. Secondly, the threat of such an 'invasion' has been aired by those media groups in the developing countries that fear that their business interests will be harmed if Western groups, equipped with large financial and technological resources and superior management skills, are allowed to operate in the country **without let**.

The fear is valid but it goes against the grain of the economic reform program. The presence of foreign newspapers and television channels will increase competition, which, in the course of time, can only lead to the upgradation of dynamic Indian newspapers and television channels, even while they drive the rest out of the market. One way to strike a balance between the two antagonistic principles would be to allow foreign media entry into the country, provided the India state treats them at par with the domestic media on all fronts. On the import of technology, for instance, foreign media cannot be allowed duty concessions denied to their Indian counterparts. Foreign media will also have to face legal consequences should they run foul of Indian laws. Why, for example, should the BBC, or Time magazine or The Economist get away by showing a map of Kashmir, which is **at variance** with the official Indian map? Why should they go scot-free when they allow secessionists and terrorists to air their views without giving the government the right to reply, or when they depict sexually explicit scenes, which would otherwise not be cleared by the Censor Board? Since the government can do precious little in the matter, especially about satellite broadcasts, what if it should consider attaching the properties of the offending parties? Demands of this kind are bound to be voiced unless New Delhi makes it clear to the foreign media that they will have to respect Indian susceptibilities, especially where it concerns the country's integrity and its culture. It may be able to derive some inspiration from France's successful attempts in the recent GATT to protect its cinematography industry.

81. Which of the following is one of the points weakening the argument to prevent the entry of foreign media?
    (a) Such entry would be against traditional culture
    (b) The threat being voiced by those whose business will be harmed by such an entry
    (c) The arguments being put forth are at loggerheads
    (d) The foreign media may not be treated on par with the domestic media
    (e) None of these

REVISION EXERCISES

82. What will be the impact of increasing competition?
    (a) The domestic media will not be able to withstand it
    (b) The foreign media will not be allowed duty concessions on import of technology
    (c) It will improve Indian newspapers and television
    (d) The Indian newspapers and news agencies will seek protection from the court
    (e) None of these
83. Which of the following has been cited as having succeeded in protecting country?
    (a) GATT
    (b) News Agencies
    (c) Television
    (d) Cultural traditions
    (e) None of these
84. Which of the following has been the major recommendation regarding the entry of foreign media?
    (a) It should not be allowed.
    (b) It should be welcomed without putting any restrictions.
    (c) Allow entry, treating them on par with domestic media.
    (d) Allow entry, provided they do not ask for duty concessions on import of technology.
    (e) None of these
85. In the controversy involving two principles regarding allowing foreign media, which of the following is against its entry?
    (a) Free flow of ideas
    (b) Preserve culture
    (c) Government restrictions
    (d) Security across national borders
    (e) Western ideology
86. According to the passage, which media in particular promotes Western interests?
    (a) American
    (b) Foreign
    (c) French
    (d) Western
    (e) None of these
87. Which of the following is the meaning of the phrase "without let", as used in the passage?
    (a) with no difficulty
    (b) without confinement
    (c) with strings
    (d) without restrictions
    (e) conducive environment
88. Why would the entry of foreign media harm local interests?
    (a) They are better equipped managerially and technologically
    (b) Our cultural heritage will be lost
    (c) Economic reform programmes will get a setback
    (d) Different sets of laws and rules were made applicable for foreign media
    (e) None of these

89. Which of the following is the meaning of the phrase "at variance", as used in the passage?
(a) discrepancy (b) at large
(c) in conformity (d) variable
(e) differing

90. Which of the following seems to be the most likely purpose of writing this passage?
(a) To criticize foreign media
(b) To highlight the exploitation by developed nations
(c) To highlight the steps and caution to be taken about the entry of foreign media
(d) To make the public aware of the technological and managerial superiority of western media
(e) To prevent foreign media from entering our country

DIRECTIONS (Qs. 91-95) : Read the following passage divided into number of paragraphs carefully and answer the questions that follow it.

Paragraph 1: Judiciary has become the centre of controversy, in the recent past, on account of the sudden 'Me' in the level of judicial intervention. The area of judicial intervention has been steadily expanding through the device of public interest litigation. The judiciary has shed its pro-status-quo approach and taken upon itself the duty to enforce the basic rights of the poor and vulnerable sections of society, by progressive interpretation and positive action. The Supreme Court has developed new methods of dispensing justice to the masses through the public interest litigation.

Paragraph 2: Former Chief Justice P. N. Bhagwati, under whose leadership public interest litigation attained a new dimension comments that "the Supreme Court has developed several new commitments. It has carried forward participative justice. It has laid just standards of procedure. It has made justice more accessible to citizens". The term 'judicial activism' is intended to refer to, and cover, the action of the court in excess of, and beyond the power of judicial review. From one angle it is said to be an act in excess of, or without, jurisdiction. The Constitution does not confer any authority or jurisdiction for 'activism' as such on the Court.

Paragraph 3: Judicial activism refers to the interference of the judiciary in the legislative and executive fields. It mainly occurs due to the non-activity of the other organs of the government. Judicial activism is a way through which relief is provided to the disadvantaged and aggrieved citizens. Judicial activism is providing a base for policy making in competition with the legislature and executive. Judicial activism is the rendering of decisions, which are in tune with the temper and tempo of the times.

Paragraph 4: In short, judicial activism means that instead of judicial restraint, the Supreme Court and other lower courts become activists and compel the authority to act and sometimes also direct the government regarding policies and also matters of administration.

REVISION EXERCISES

Paragraph 5: Judicial activism has arisen mainly due to the failure of the executive and legislatures to act. Secondly, it has arisen also due to the fact that there is a doubt that the legislature and executive have failed to deliver the goods. Thirdly, it occurs because the entire system has been plagued by ineffectiveness and inactiveness. The violation of basic human rights has also led to judicial activism. Finally, due to the misuse and abuse of some of the provisions of the Constitution, judicial activism has gained significance.

91. What does the author want to convey in Paragraph 1?
    (I) Certain personal issues and agendas in recent past in the level of judicial intervention have put a question mark on the credibility of the apex court.
    (II) The Supreme Court is very concerned about the under-privileged sections of the society and thus, has come up with an innovative idea to dispensing justice.
    (III) Public Interest Litigation is a boon for the poor and vulnerable sections of the society as far as the enforcement of their basic rights is concerned.
    (a) Only (I)   (b) Only (II)
    (c) Both (II) and (III)   (d) All (I), (II) and (III)
    (e) None of these

92. What is the meaning of the sentence 'From one angle, it is said to be an act in excess of, or without jurisdiction' in the context of paragraph 2?
    (I) Judicial activism can be exercised by the Supreme Court as it is beyond the power of judicial review.
    (II) Judicial activism does not find any mention in the constitution as far as its authority or jurisdiction is concerned.
    (III) The constitution has not limited the authority or jurisdiction to 'activism' hence, it can be exercised over the courts as per the say of the Supreme Court.
    (a) Only (I)   (b) Only (II)
    (c) Only (III)   (d) Both (II) and (III)
    (e) Both (I) and (II)

93. What can't be said about judicial activism in accordance to paragraph 3?
    (a) It emerges when the legislative and the judiciary do not do justice with their work.
    (b) It has the right to put question mark on the legislative and executive part of the government.
    (c) It is exercised in accordance with the demand of the situation.
    (d) It has given the citizenry ample power to demand for their rights from the judiciary.
    (e) It is giving a foundation for policy making in competition with the other organs of the government.

94. Which of the following statements does not relate to Paragraph 5?
    (a) Violation of basic human rights has led to judicial activism.
    (b) There is a suspicion on the executive and the legislative organ of the government as far as their working is concerned.
    (c) Judicial activism has carried forward participative justice thereby justifying that the entire system has been plagued by ineffectiveness and inactiveness.
    (d) Some of the constitutional provisions have been misused.
    (e) The failure of the other organs of the government has led to the emergence of judicial activism.
95. What does the author mean by the phrase '**judicial restraint**' in Paragraph 4?
    (I) The limiting of the exercise of their own power by the courts.
    (II) The restriction of power which Supreme Court can impose on other lower courts.
    (III) The liberation of judicial power of the Supreme Court and other courts.
    (a) Only (I) (b) Only (II)
    (c) Only (III) (d) Both (I) and (II)
    (e) All (I), (II) and (II)

DIRECTIONS (Qs. 96-100) : Read the following passage divided into number of paragraphs carefully and answer the questions that follow it.

Paragraph 1: India is land of Diversity. Our country has various languages, religion, culture, tradition etc. various elements of Indian culture such as Indian books on philosophy, Indian cuisine, yoga etc. have created an impact all over the world. Western culture is also called European civilization, Western civilization or Western lifestyle. It is based on certain belief, systems, traditional customs, moral and ethical values. The term not only applies to European countries but to places where we see spread of European culture.

Paragraph 2: India is a country rich in its heritage and culture, but we are seeing fading of Indian culture at many places of India, especially at the urban societies of India. The effect of western culture is greatly seen in our customs, tradition, social and moral behavior, our love and respect for others. These days a person loves to live in freedom, he does not want to bind themselves in Indian customs and traditions. Day by day we see breaking of joint family and more and more development of nuclear family.

Paragraph 3: Very few are interested in making adjustments and share their things with other family members, the word privacy is given greater importance and the love and respect towards other especially elders are decreasing day by day. In this information age people are too busy to care for others. Western culture has brought with it the seeds of selfishness in the minds of Indian.

Paragraph 4: These are contradictory to Indian culture which has always taught to live in harmony with each other and always love and respect everyone at home.

REVISION EXERCISES

With lack in experience of a nuclear family due to the absence of grandfather and grandmother, and both parents working a child fails to learn ethical or moral values, and learn whatever little he sees and understands from the world and his teachers. In this way we end up bringing up a child who has little ethical values and do not hesitate in doing any unfair practices, because no one is there to teach him good or bad or stop him from doing something bad.

Paragraph 5: We should know what is right and wrong for us. Western culture is not altogether bad, although it has made our life faster but enhanced technology has also made our life easier and comfortable. We need to give importance to our Indian culture which taught us to live in peace and harmony with other by way of increasing our tolerance and patience. Many people of other countries are realizing the importance of Indian heritage and are adapting the goodness of Indian culture such as practice of Yoga and meditation, wisdom and teachings passed by the ancient saints. The knowledge of Indian wisdom helps human being of any race to enrich their life.

96. Why is Western culture also known as European culture as given in paragraph1?
    (I) Because it has created impact all over the western countries.
    (II) Because it is based on certain belief, systems, traditional customs, moral and ethical values.
    (III) Because Europe is located in the western part of the earth.
    (a) Only (I) (b) Only (II)
    (c) Only (III) (d) Both (I) and (II)
    (e) None of the three

97. How according to the author has Western culture impacted India in Paragraph 2?
    (I) Modern Indians, in the contemporary era do not value their customs and traditions.
    (II) Western culture has impacted Indian culture adversely.
    (III) Western construct is liked by the Indians very much and they are practising it in full swing.
    (a) Only (I) (b) Only (II)
    (c) Both (I) and (II) (d) Both (II) and (III)
    (e) All (I), (II) and (III)

98. What can be inferred by the phrase '**In this information age**' as given in Paragraph 3?
    (I) In today's world, information is transferred from one person to another very fast.
    (II) This is the era of technological advancement.
    (III) Betterment of technology has led to faster mode of accessing information.
    (a) Only (I) (b) Only (II)
    (c) Both (II) and (III) (d) All (I), (II) and (III)
    (e) None of the three

99. Which of the following words is opposite to the meaning of the word '**ethical**' as used in Paragraph 4?
    (I) Virtuous
    (II) Kosher
    (III) Humane
    (a) Only (I)   (b) Only (II)
    (c) Only (III)   (d) All (I), (II) and (III)
    (e) None of the three

100. What has been delineated in Paragraph 5?
    (I) The author is sceptical about Western culture.
    (II) Though Western culture has impacted India but, Indian culture has an edge over it as many people of other countries are realizing the importance of Indian heritage and are adapting the goodness of Indian culture such as practice of Yoga and meditation, wisdom and teachings passed by the ancient saints.
    (III) Western culture has changed our lifestyle.
    (a) Only (I)   (b) Only (II)
    (c) Only (III)   (d) Both (II) and (III)
    (e) None of these

PARAJUMBLES

101. If Sentence (C), "There appears to be no end in sight to the cycle of boom and bust in the prices of agricultural goods." is the first sentence, what is the order of other sentences after rearrangement?

    A. Curiously, potato prices were many times higher just months ago amid scarce supply.
    B. With the price of a kilogram of potato dropping as low as under a rupee in certain wholesale markets, many distressed farmers have left their produce to rot on the roads, and in cold storage facilities.
    C. There appears to be no end in sight to the cycle of boom and bust in the prices of agricultural goods.
    D. Over the last few weeks, across India the price of potatoes has fallen sharply after a year of bumper production.
    E. Last year, the price of other produce like red chilli, tur dal and tomato witnessed a similar trend of steep falls compared to the previous season.
    F. The sharp swing in prices has been explained by the Cobweb phenomenon.
    (a) EDABF   (b) EFADB
    (c) DABEF   (d) DBAEF
    (e) BDAEF

REVISION EXERCISES

102. If Sentence (C), "Ever since the price of bitcoins skyrocketed from a little under $1,000 (around ₹63,400 now) in 2016 to touch nearly $20,000 last year, people have been posing a Hamlet kind of question: to buy or not to buy? " is the first sentence, what is the order of other sentences after rearrangement?
    A. Some have explicitly warned investors to exercise caution while those like the Indian government have begun imposing a tax on the gains from the sale of bitcoins.
    B. Their dilemma is understandable.
    C. Ever since the price of bitcoins skyrocketed from a little under $1,000 (around ₹63,400 now) in 2016 to touch nearly $20,000 last year, people have been posing a Hamlet kind of question: to buy or not to buy?
    D. On the other hand, there is the nagging feeling that one may end up investing in a virtual currency whose price is extremely volatile and whose true value cannot be assessed.
    E. Adding to the confusion, most governments remain non-committal on the legality of bitcoins since it is not regulated by central banks.
    F. On the one hand, there is the fear of losing out on an opportunity to make money hand over fist by investing or trading in bitcoins since their price rose by around 20-fold since the start of 2017.
    (a) BFDAE (b) BFAED
    (c) BFDEA (d) FDBEA
    (e) FDEBA

103. If Sentence (C), "There is one strong message from the findings of the Annual Status of Education Report (Rural) 2017, it is that the Right of Children to Free and Compulsory Education Act should cover the entire spectrum of 18 years, and not confine itself to those aged 6 to 14. " is the first sentence, what is the order of other sentences after rearrangement?
    A. Guaranteed inclusion will empower those in the 14-18 age group who are not enrolled anywhere, and help them acquire finishing education that is so vital to their participation in the workforce.
    B. It is absolutely essential for all of them to get an education that equips them with the skills, especially job-oriented vocational capabilities,
    C. There is one strong message from the findings of the Annual Status of Education Report (Rural) 2017, it is that the Right of Children to Free and Compulsory Education Act should cover the entire spectrum of 18 years, and not confine itself to those aged 6 to 14.
    D. Unfortunately, the state of rural elementary education is far from encouraging.
    E. if the expectation of a demographic dividend is to be meaningful.
    F. The ASER sample study estimates that 14% of this age group — a total of 125 million young Indians in this category — are not enrolled.
    (a) AFBED (b) BEAFD
    (c) DAFBE (d) AFEBD
    (e) FABED

104. If Sentence (F), "The sharp rise in bond yields has hit banks with losses on treasury operations dominated by sovereign bond holdings." is the first sentence, what is the order of other sentences after rearrangement?

A. The yield on Indian 10-year benchmark government bonds has risen steeply, from about 6.5% at the end of August to 7.56% on January 16.

B. Bankers have pleaded that the Reserve Bank of India allow them to stagger the reporting of these losses over several quarters.

C. Rating agency ICRA believes the fall in bond prices on expectation of the Central government breaching its fiscal deficit target has led to banks suffering a loss on paper of over Rs.15,500 crore in the quarter that ended in December.

D. In seeking leeway, they have pointed to the huge burden imposed on their balance sheets by non-performing assets clogging the banking system.

E. Even the yield on newly issued 10-year bonds that would mature in 2028 has inched up 27 basis points since January 5.

F. The sharp rise in bond yields has hit banks with losses on treasury operations dominated by sovereign bond holdings.

(a) ABECD (b) ABCED
(c) CAEBD (d) BCADE
(e) CEBAD

105. If Sentence (F), "The winter session of Parliament saw more political positioning than appraisal of a legislation to make instant triple talaq a criminal offence. " is the first sentence, what is the order of other sentences after rearrangement?

A. The Opposition has raised three concerns: whether a civil wrong, mainly a breach of a marriage contract in an arbitrary manner, ought to be treated as a crime; whether it is not a contradiction of sorts for the law to jail a husband for pronouncing instant talaq and also mandate that he pay a subsistence allowance to the wife; and whether making it a cognizable and non-bailable offence would lead to it being misused against Muslim men.

B. Further, some see an internal contradiction in the way the law is sought to be framed.

C. The core question is whether resorting to an illegal and arbitrary form of divorce should necessarily lead to a prison term for the offending husband.

D. With the Muslim Women (Protection of Rights on Marriage) Bill pending in the Rajya Sabha, the best option would be to refer it to a select committee to help bring about a consensus on how to address the problem of talaq-e-biddat

E. A three-year prison term, besides a fine, also raises the issue of proportionality.

REVISION EXERCISES

F. The winter session of Parliament saw more political positioning than appraisal of a legislation to make instant triple talaq a criminal offence.
(a) ABCED (b) EDCBA
(c) CDAEB (d) DABCE
(e) DCEAB

106. If sentence (C) "The decision to use Aadhaar as proof of identity in the annual collation of data on teachers employed in higher education has led to an uncomfortable discovery: nearly a tenth of them turned out to be ghost teachers." is the first sentence, what is the order of other sentences after rearrangement?

(A) Around 130,000 teachers were found to be fake.
(B) The human resource development (HRD) ministry in 2017 told colleges and universities across India that while furnishing data they need to give the Aadhaar number of the faculty members to authenticate their presence.
(C) The decision to use Aadhaar as proof of identity in the annual collation of data on teachers employed in higher education has led to an uncomfortable discovery: nearly a tenth of them turned out to be ghost teachers.
(D) the bad news is that the country has just found out that understaffing in higher education institutes is far greater than what has been estimated so far.
(E) While the good news is that this will lead to a focus on improving the quality of teaching,
(F) India has about 1.4 million teachers in colleges and universities.
(a) DFAEB (b) BAFDE
(c) BEDAF (d) AFEDB
(e) DAEFB

107. If sentence (C) "The Reserve Bank of India will shortly issue new ₹ 10 notes under the Mahatma Gandhi series." is the first sentence, what is the order of other sentences after rearrangement?

(A) With chocolate brown colour as the base, the new note will bear the picture of Konark Sun Temple.
(B) The central bank has already printed around 1 billion pieces of the new ₹ 10 note.
(C) The Reserve Bank of India will shortly issue new ₹ 10 notes under the Mahatma Gandhi series.
(D) The change in design in the old ₹ 10 note was last made in 2005.
(E) The design received the go-ahead from the government last week, said the two of the people cited earlier.
(F) In August last year, RBI had introduced the new ₹ 200 and ₹ 50 notes under the Mahatma Gandhi series.
(a) DFAEB (b) AEFDB
(c) FEDAB (d) BDEFA
(e) BAEDF

REVISION EXERCISES

108. If sentence (C) "The continuing failure of the Myanmar government to act decisively and urgently to protect civilians from the raging crossfire between the security forces and insurgents is shocking." is the first sentence, what is the order of other sentences after rearrangement?
   (A) The latest flare-up began last Friday when militants suspected to be from the Arakan Rohingya Salvation Army attacked military and police outposts.
   (B) That should have served as a caution against an excessive counter-insurgency operation, a real possibility given the history of systematic persecution of the Muslim minorities in Rakhine.
   (C) The continuing failure of the Myanmar government to act decisively and urgently to protect civilians from the raging crossfire between the security forces and insurgents is shocking.
   (D) Most of the victims are women and children, according to the UN's International Organisation for Migration, which has called for additional aid to cope with Dhaka's refugee situation.
   (E) The military crackdown that followed has been widely condemned as disproportionate and the government accused of being an onlooker.
   (F) The recent clashes in the western State of Rakhine have claimed over 70 lives and forced thousands of Rohingya to flee across the border into Bangladesh, in a rapidly deteriorating humanitarian crisis.
   (a) DAFEB   (b) FDABE
   (c) FEDBA   (d) BDEAF
   (e) BEDFA

109. If sentence (C) "The success of the first developmental flight of GSLV Mark III will enable indigenous launching up to 4 tonne class of communication satellites in the future." is the first sentence, what is the order of other sentences after rearrangement?
   (A) Next developmental launch is in first half of 2018.
   (B) ISRO has been providing commercial launch services for earth observation satellites and small satellites onboard the Polar Satellite Launch Vehicle (PSLV) through Antrix Corporation Limited since 1999.
   (C) The success of the first developmental flight of GSLV Mark III will enable indigenous launching up to 4 tonne class of communication satellites in the future.
   (D) The successful launch of GSLV Mark III is a step ahead in building credibility in launching.
   (E) Some more launches of GSLV-MK III will be needed before GSLV MK III gets recognised internationally as a vehicle for transportation to space.
   (F) ISRO has just completed one launch of GSLV-MK III.
   (a) BDFAE   (b) FBEDA
   (c) FEDBA   (d) AEDBF
   (e) BFADE

REVISION EXERCISES

110. If sentence (C) "The Central Government is the competent authority to initiate disciplinary proceedings against IAS officers for misconducts while working in the affairs of Government of India." is the first sentence, what is the order of other sentences after rearrangement?

(A) The Central Government is also the competent authority in respect of disciplinary proceedings initiated by the State Government where subsequent to inquiry, a major penalty has been proposed.

(B) The Central Government also considers proposals for sanction for prosecution against IAS Officers for offences under P.C. Act, 1988, subsequent to completion of investigation and filing of chargesheet.

(C) The Central Government is the competent authority to initiate disciplinary proceedings against IAS officers for misconducts while working in the affairs of Government of India.

(D) Department of Post and Telegraph in exercise of powers conferred under sub-rule 3 of the Rule 16 of the All India Services (Death-cum-retirement Benefits) Rules 1958 has prematurely retired, in public interest, 4 (four) IAS officers since 2014.

(E) There are 36 disciplinary proceeding against IAS officers (State and Central cases) currently in progress at various stages.

(F) In the past one year 8 cases for prosecution sanction have been granted by the Central Government.

(a) AEDBF (b) FADBE
(c) FEDBA (d) AEBFD
(e) BFADE

IDIOMS & PHRASES

DIRECTIONS (Qs. 111-120) : In the following questions, a part of the sentence is given in bold, it is then followed by three sentences which try to explain the meaning of the phrase given in bold. Choose the best set of alternatives from the five options given below each question which explains the meaning of the phrase correctly without altering the meaning of the sentence given as question.

111. **The dichotomy is the striking feature.** An estimated 20 per cent of our population is economically advanced with access to the latest technology, while the rest wallows in inhuman conditions

(I) The contrast can clearly be understood by the fact that an estimated one-fifth of our population is economically sound with access to the latest technology while the rest are still in critical condition.

(II) It is quite attractive that around 20 per cent of our population has access to the latest technology unlike the rest of the population thereby, contributing more in the economic development.

(III) It is shameful that the majority of our population is unaware of advanced technology and thus, they are not able to compete with the technologically advanced people of our country.
- (a) Only (I) is correct
- (b) Only (III) is correct
- (c) Both (II) and (III) are correct
- (d) Both (I) and (III) are correct
- (e) None is correct

112. It may have taken 20 years to develop the export market for UK garden furniture, but if there is to be a price war, **the industry could be back to square one within** 12 months.
   - (I) It took two decades to develop the export market for UK garden furniture, however, in case of high competition among its peers, it will always emerge victorious and that too within 1 year.
   - (II) The development of the export market of UK garden furniture took 20 years and it has reached to such a position that in case of price war, it can defeat all other industries within 12 months.
   - (III) Despite 20 years of hard work done to develop the export market of UK garden furniture, still the industry is sceptical about it success. It may fall down in case of a price war.
   - (a) Only (I) is correct   (b) Only (II) is correct
   - (c) Only (III) is correct   (d) Both (I) and (II) are correct
   - (e) None is correct

113. As the situation got out of control during the match, **the captain of the team tried to put oil over troubled waters.**
   - (I) Seeing the situation going out of control, the captain of the team tried to calm down the players.
   - (II) As the situation was out of control, the captain of the team had no other option than to support his teammates and fight with the opposition.
   - (III) Taking advantage of the bad situation, the captain of the team too argued along with his teammates and tried to worsen the situation.
   - (a) Only (I) is correct   (b) Only (II) is correct
   - (c) Only (III) is correct   (d) Both (II) and (III) are correct
   - (e) None is correct

114. **The manager had to eat a humble pie** after the workers decided to go on strike to protest against the biased salary hike and promotions.
   - (I) The manager politely refused to take his decision back despite knowing that the employees would go for a strike against the nepotism in salary hike and promotions.
   - (II) Seeing the urgency of the situation and the threat of strike given by the workers, the manager withdrew his decision of giving salary hike and promotions to his favourite employees.

REVISION EXERCISES

(III) Knowing the fact that the employees would go for a strike against the biased salary hike and promotions, the manager gave up his pride and apologized for his mistake.

(a) Only (I) is correct (b) Only (II) is correct
(c) Only (III) is correct (d) Both (II) and (III) are correct
(e) None is correct

115. The teacher tried his best to explain the importance of the chapter to the students but soon realized that he **was casting pearls before swine.**

(I) The teacher soon realized that whatever he was explaining to the students about the chapter was grasped by them the way he expected.

(II) Despite the hard work done by the teacher to explain the importance of the chapter, the students were busy making mockery of him.

(III) After trying his best to make the students understand the importance of the chapter, the teacher soon realized that they are not recognising its worth.

(a) Only (I) is correct (b) Only (II) is correct
(c) Only (III) is correct (d) Both (II) and (III) are correct
(e) None is correct

116. Any curb on access to higher education, for instance, **would run counter to the prevailing mood** among the middle class, which wants further improvements to the overall standard of living.

(I) Any restriction on access to higher education would barely affect the mood of the middle class which expects further improvements to the overall standard of living.

(II) The present spirit of the middle class which wants further improvements to the overall standard of living will worsen if the access to higher education is paused for any reason.

(III) Any clampdown on the access to higher education is likely to alter the mood of the middle class which wants further improvements to the overall standard of living.

(a) Only (I) is correct (b) Only (II) is correct
(c) Only (III) is correct (d) Both (II) and (III) are correct
(e) None is correct

117. We were all set for the picnic but the sudden change in the plan by my dad to go for the movie instead of picnic came **out of the blue.**

(I) The sudden change in the plan to go for the movie instead of picnic was a well thought idea by my dad.

(II) The sudden change made in the plan by my father to go for the movie instead of picnic was unexpected for us.

(III) My dad had already made his mind to change the plan to go for the movie instead of picnic, however, we had intuitions about the change.
(a) Only (I) is correct   (b) Only (II) is correct
(c) Only (III) is correct   (d) Both (I) and (III) are correct
(e) None is correct

118. The Supreme Court has **struck a blow for the rights of the disabled,** with a direction to the Central and State governments to provide full access to public facilities, such as buildings and transport, within stipulated deadlines.
   (I) The Supreme Court has ordered all the states to provide full access to public facilities like building and transport to the disabled and they must not ignore the true spirit and purpose of the law made for these people.
   (II) The Supreme Court has ordered the central government to provide the basic amenities to the disabled within the stipulated time period.
   (III) The Supreme Court has warned the Central and State governments for the rights of the disabled which they are deprived of and has ordered them to provide full access to public facilities, such as buildings and transport, within stipulated deadlines.
   (a) Only (I) is correct   (b) Only (II) is correct
   (c) Only (III) is correct   (d) All are correct
   (e) None is correct

119. At the UN General Assembly, USA and India accused Pakistan of funding terrorism in South-East Asia but **Pakistan kept on beating around the bush.**
   (I) USA and India accused Pakistan of funding terrorism in South-East Asia at the UN General Assembly however, Pakistan kept on refusing it.
   (II) Pakistan was accused of funding terrorism in South-East Asia at the UN General Assembly by India and USA but Pakistan kept on avoiding this topic.
   (III) The rising terror in the South-East Asia was the major concern at the UN General Assembly. USA and India accused Pakistan of funding terrorism in the area which was partially accepted by Pakistan.
   (a) Only (I) is correct   (b) Only (II) is correct
   (c) Only (III) is correct   (d) All are correct
   (e) None is correct

120. **Manish was in doldrums** after he was badly scolded by the teacher in front of all the students.
   (I) Manish was in huge anger after being badly scolded by the teacher in front of all the students.
   (II) Manish felt so insulted after being badly scolded by the teacher in front of all his colleagues that he started planning to take the revenge of the insult.
   (III) Manish was depressed after he was badly scolded by the teacher in front of all the students.
   (a) Only (I) is correct   (b) Only (II) is correct
   (c) Only (III) is correct   (d) Both (I) and (II) are correct
   (e) None is correct

REVISION EXERCISES

SENTENCE FILLERS

DIRECTIONS (Qs. 121-130): In each of the following questions, a paragraph with a blank is given. From the five choices given below, select the sentence which can go into the blank to make the paragraph logically coherent.

121. Srinagar is the capital of Kashmir. There are very beautiful scenes all round. The Dal Lake is one among them. [_____] We can hire one of them and voyage along the length and breadth of the lake or live in it for a week or so.
    (a) There are several guides to take us round.
    (b) There, we can see a number of house boats waiting to be hired by the tourists.
    (c) It is difficult to count them.
    (d) It was dark inside and bright outside.
    (e) There are several tourists looking around the place.

122. Polio-affected children are found everywhere in India. Recently, the Government has started Polio-eradication Scheme. [_____] Unless we take care to co-operate, the purpose cannot be fulfilled.
    (a) We must help children to take the proper vaccine.
    (b) We must take the children to get vaccinated.
    (c) Children must remain without any movement.
    (d) We must make children exercise.
    (e) We need experts to undertake such projects.

123. Many film-stars have recently migrated to the area of television. [_____] As the viewers increase their popularity also increases. T.V serials appear to be more paying than the feature films.
    (a) Television gives a better chance of action.
    (b) There they have a greater number of viewers.
    (c) Television is a house hold affair.
    (d) If we do not like a TV program we can turn it off.
    (e) Television is useful in many ways.

124. Man is trying to find out modern means of producing electric power. The solar panel is one of them. [_____] This electricity can light lamps, turn fans or work small household appliances.
    (a) It is very cheap and affordable.
    (b) We ourselves can make one such device.
    (c) It converts sunlight into electricity.
    (d) It is easy to work and beautiful to look at.
    (e) Electricity is a good substitute for sunlight.

125. Air-pollution is one of the gravest problems faced by city-dwellers. Foul gas liberated from heaps of waste matter is one source of pollution. [_____] Recently, the Government has made arrangements to measure it. If it is above the allowable limit, the vehicles will be prohibited from plying along the public roads.

(a) Another source is the smoke emitted by vehicles.
(b) Foul water in the channels is another.
(c) The smell from toddy shops pollutes the air.
(d) Open drainage pollutes the air.
(e) People suffer due to smoke emitted by vehicles.

126. Providing benefits for women on maternity leave and children is a societal responsibility which can be funded in a large country through a combination of general taxation and contributory payments from those who have the means. Health care should be treated as a right and deliveries handled without cost to women. _____ Such a policy would harmonise the varying maternity benefit provisions found in different laws that govern labour at present.

(a) The income guarantees during the pregnancy period can be ensured through a universal social insurance system.
(b) Beneficiaries covered by the latest amendment must be protected from discrimination through clear provisions.
(c) Mandating creche facilities to help women workers under the changed law is a forward-looking move.
(d) Women's empowerment can be achieved through universal initiatives, not by imposing conditionalities to avail benefits.
(e) Access to welfare support has become even more critical as workers migrate frequently due to economic changes.

127. Fringe elements affiliated with the BJP have been in the news ever since the party came to power. Activists who pretend to be associated with the Trinamool Congress in West Bengal and the Samajwadi Party in Uttar Pradesh too have had their day in the news. _____. First, the "fringe" is encouraged by the party as a strategy to appeal to more extreme elements within the party and to polarise politics. Second, and more specific to the right wing, some believe that these individuals' provocative actions and remarks are indicative of the government's tacit support for Hindutva principles.

(a) There are two reasons of the palpable polarization in politics.
(b) There are also local politicians who have misperceived favourable responses or miscalculated the impacts of their actions.
(c) There are two widely held explanations for such activism.
(d) In our view, this results from a systemic problem with our politics.
(e) Their two actions have served to embarrass the BJP and the Central government.

REVISION EXERCISES 173

128. Traditional pharmacies have been knocking at the doors of the government for some time now as they face intense competition from e-pharmacies. Their profit margins and market share have faced pressure in recent years from e-pharmacies that often offer medicines at cheaper prices. _____. The AIOCD has repeatedly accused e-pharmacies of a wide range of malpractices, including selling fake drugs and enabling self-medication. The organisation has been citing these issues to seek a ban on the sale of drugs online.

    (a) While this has improved the accessibility of drugs to a wider population, the concern of traditional pharmacists too is easy to understand.
    (b) The Ministry of Health and Family Welfare proposed the setting up of an e-portal to track and regulate the sale of drugs across the retail chain.
    (c) The risks associated with e-pharmacies, especially when it comes to the dispensation of prescription drugs without the necessary checks, cannot be taken lightly.
    (d) However, the Ministry's plan on regulating e-pharmacies is a rather outdated one.
    (e) But perhaps the only thing clear from the All India Organisation of Chemists and Druggists (AIOCD)'s demands is its intention to protect the business interests of traditional brick-and-mortar pharmacies

129. With the direction of global headwinds remaining uncertain, growth in government spending budgeted to be lower this year compared to last year, and private investment virtually absent, the lowering GDP numbers should serve as a reality check. _____. While the government has vigorously underlined its reform achievements of the last three years, such as the Goods and Services Tax that rolls out in July, a mission-mode reform reboot is urgently needed and that can only begin if the problem is suitably acknowledged by policymakers.

    (a) While lower inflation and growth may soften the RBI's outlook, there is little that monetary policy alone can do at this juncture to revive animal spirits.
    (b) Returning to the 8% growth mark is going to be a big challenge.
    (c) In fact, the only reason the 7.1% estimate has held up is because growth for the previous quarters was revised upwards.
    (d) Private consumption grew at the slowest pace in five quarters, even as construction and manufacturing activities dipped sharply.
    (e) Yet, whichever way one looks at it, the note ban seems to have exacerbated the problem, particularly for India's large informal economy that the poor depend on, as even the World Bank has now noted.

REVISION EXERCISES

130. The United States currently gives an impression of being at war with itself. This stems from a series of charges and countercharges levied against President Donald Trump and his advisers, including that of collusion with the Russians, who are accused of meddling with the presidential election. _____. Meanwhile, the kaleidoscopic nature of the changes taking place in the top echelons of the new administration is hardly helping matters. The peremptory actions of the president, such as the dismissal of Federal Bureau of Investigation Director James Comey, have only aggravated this situation. Almost every step taken by the new administration is leading to partisan rows.
   (a) One of the principal charges against members of the Trump team is that they maintained improper contact with Russian diplomats.
   (b) The media and intelligence agencies are far from impartial in their behaviour.
   (c) Several probes have already been launched in this connection.
   (d) Barack Obama, Mr. Trump's predecessor, is by contrast credited currently with many more virtues than at any time when he was in office.
   (e) What has led to a fractured society in the U.S. today carries a message for democracies everywhere.

EVALUATING INFERENCE

DIRECTIONS (Qs. 131-140) : In each of the given questions, an inference is given in bold which is then followed by three paragraphs. You have to find the paragraph(s) from where it is inferred. Choose the option with the best possible outcome as your choice.

131. **Triple talaq is banned now**
   (I) The Supreme Court said triple talaq violates the fundamental rights of Muslim women as it irrevocably ends marriage without any chance of reconciliation. Triple talaq, or verbal divorce, is practiced by some in the Muslim community to instantly divorce their wives by saying talaq three times.
   (II) By ruling the discriminatory practice of instant triple talaq as unconstitutional **and unlawful**, the Supreme Court has sent out a clear message that personal law can no longer be privileged over fundamental rights. Three of the five judges on the Constitution Bench have not accepted the argument that instant talaq, or *talaq-e-biddat*, is essential to Islam and, therefore, deserves constitutional protection under Article 25.
   (III) The Centre's proposal to make instant triple talaq an offence punishable with three-year imprisonment and a fine is an unnecessary attempt to convert a civil wrong into a criminal act. By a three-two majority, the Supreme Court has already declared, and correctly, that the practice of talaq-e-biddat, or instant divorce of a Muslim woman by uttering the word 'talaq' thrice, is illegal and unenforceable.

REVISION EXERCISES

(a) Only (I) is correct (b) Only (II) is correct
(c) Only (III) is correct (d) Both (II) and (III) are correct
(e) All are correct

132. It is good to invest in Bitcoin
  (I) India's policy on Bitcoin regulation is still evolving and no legal framework exists. The RBI has cautioned against its use, informing users, holders, investors and traders dealing with virtual currencies that they are doing so at their own risk.
  (II) One lakh rupees invested in bitcoin in 2010 would be worth a few hundred crore rupees today. That is the kind of extraordinary return the digital currency has given investors as its price has witnessed a meteoric rise, from just a few cents in 2010 to hit a lifetime high of over $11,000 last week.
  (III) Even if you become a bitcoin miner, there is no guarantee that you would be able to mine a certain number of bitcoins. Any scheme related to bitcoins promising a fixed return is likely a tall promise best avoided.
  (a) Only (I) is correct (b) Only (II) is correct
  (c) Only (III) is correct (d) Both (II) and (III) are correct
  (e) All are correct

133. Cyber security is a major concern for country like India
  (I) India is one of the key players in the digital and knowledge-based economy, holding more than a 50% share of the world's outsourcing market. Pioneering and technology-inspired programmes such as Aadhaar, MyGov, Government e-Market, DigiLocker, Bharat Net, Startup India, Skill India and Smart Cities are propelling India towards technological competence and transformation. India is already the third largest hub for technology-driven startups in the world and its Information and Communications Technology sector is estimated to reach the $225 billion landmark by 2020.
  (II) To encourage development of new technologies in the field of cyber security, the Ministry of Electronics and Information Technology will offer challenge grants of up to Rs 5 crore to start-ups to spur research and development, Minister for Electronics and IT said on the previous day. "We are in the process of working with Data Security Council of India to conduct challenge grant for cyber security…," the Minister added.
  (III) Two things set aside India's digital spaces from that of major powers such as the United States and China: design and density. India is a net information exporter. Its information highways point west, carrying with them the data of millions of Indians. This is not a design flaw, but simply reflects the popularity of social media platforms and the lack of any serious effort by the Indian government to restrict the flow of data.
  (a) Only (I) is correct (b) Only (II) is correct
  (c) Only (III) is correct (d) Both (II) and (III) are correct
  (e) None is correct

134. Demonetisation has benefitted the Indian Economy
  (I) While the jury is still out on whether last year's demonetisation has harmed the Indian economy, the government's Chief Statistician maintains that the picture will become clear in the current fiscal only after data from the government and company accounts come in. He maintains he has reservations about "making quick" judgements about the note ban decision that had affected the economy at multiple levels, and that it should not be seen just from the perspective of cash replacement, but as one that produced many benefits too.
  (II) Listing out the advantages of demonetisation, Union Finance Minister said that direct tax collections had risen 15.7% till September 18, adding that undisclosed income of ₹ 5,400 crore was also detected. "Net collections up to September 18 in the current financial year rose to ₹ 3.7 lakh crore, a growth of 15.7%. The revenue collections in case of direct taxes rose to ₹ 8,49,818 crore during 2016-17, a growth of 14.5%," he said.
  (III) Indian Economy has witnessed close to 20% decline in currency in circulation, number of tax payers has considerably increased and a large number of shell companies have been identified.
  (a) Only (I) is correct   (b) Only (II) is correct
  (c) Only (III) is correct   (d) Both (II) and (III) are correct
  (e) All are correct
135. The government is trying hard to lure FDI in India
  (I) In yet another significant move to attract Foreign Direct Investment (FDI), the government has opened the door wider in several major sectors of the Indian economy, through what it calls "path-breaking" amendments in the extant FDI policy.
  (II) In less than a year, the Government of India has announced yet another set of "radical changes" in foreign direct investment (FDI) policies. The earlier announcement in November 2015 introduced changes in 15 major sectors, and the latest announcement covers nine sectors which seek to further simplify the regulations governing FDI in the country and make India an attractive destination for foreign investors".
  (III) For India, the servicing burden of FDI in terms of repatriations, dividend payments and payments for use of intellectual property is now showing up prominently. About half of the inflows into India during the past six years were balanced by outflows.
  (a) Only (I) is correct   (b) Only (II) is correct
  (c) Only (III) is correct   (d) Both (I) and (II) are correct
  (e) All are correct
136. Does India need Bullet Trains?
  (I) The proposed bullet train project is just a piece of stone that has been laid by our Prime Minister and Japanese premier, but it has already been written off as a white elephant by most analysts and commentators. They are probably right. The project, of course, is alarmingly expensive.

REVISION EXERCISES

(II) The government had set an ambitious deadline to complete the bullet train project on August 15, 2022 when India marked 75 years of Independence. The project will be executed through a special purpose vehicle, the National High Speed Rail Corporation Ltd. "The bullet train project will take care of high speed, high growth and high-end technology," Mr. Modi said, describing it as "a symbol of New India" that his government wants to build by 2022.

(III) Bullet train in India is a vanity project which has little or no justification on the grounds of economic viability or public service. Even the vanity angle — looking to position India among the ranks of developed countries — is a huge overreach. Only a handful of high-income countries with specific demographics have high-speed rail (HSR), while many have failed in their efforts, others have abandoned it after studying it. The main problem is viability, given the huge costs involved.

(a) Only (I) is correct (b) Only (II) is correct
(c) Only (III) is correct (d) Both (I) and (III) are correct
(e) All are correct

137. Indian art and culture is far ahead from Western art and culture

(I) Art in India is still very European centric. Why isn't Indian art given its due importance? "Indian art is spiritual, but it has nothing to do with any particular sect. A common misconception among society is that Indian art is religious. "The two should not be confused. It is more spiritual and less about rituals. For instance, the character Krishna means so many things. It is more of a symbol than just a god." Similarly, Arjuna is not just the character Arjuna, when depicted in a painting. He represents valour, action and mind.

(II) Assertive cultural pride is understandable, even justified only when a group is breaking away from prolonged cultural subjugation and humiliation, as was the case in mid-19th century India, when profound distortions were introduced by cultural imperialism in our self-understandings. But already by early 20th century, in the expressions of Vivekananda, Tagore and Gandhi, we see an articulation of legitimate cultural pride that behoves a confident cultural community. What then is the need for such vociferous assertion now?

(III) During the peak of the trade in mid-17th century, millions of yards of Indian cloth were being sold in markets as far as Japan, Africa, Middle-East and Europe. India's central location in the Indian Ocean basin was ideal for trading textiles to both East and West, with Gujarat, the Coromandel Coast and Bengal being the major trading centres.

(a) Only (I) is correct (b) Only (II) is correct
(c) Only (III) is correct (d) Both (I) and (III) are correct
(e) None is correct

138. The Doklam issue between India and China no more exists
   (I) The resolution of the Sino-Indian military stand-off at Doklam, that lasted close to two and a half months, is a much-awaited and welcome development where patient statecraft and deft diplomacy seem to have paid off. Even as several significant questions remain unanswered about the terms and conditions of the resolution, it provides New Delhi and Beijing an opportunity to reflect over what went wrong and rejig this important bilateral relationship.
   (II) Our Prime Minister at the BRICS summit was confident that the resolution of two-month old Doklam stand-off between the People's Liberation Army (PLA) and the Indian Army in Bhutan has gone into annals of military history. The resolution of the Doklam stand-off has now become a case study on how to deal with China, the rising global power, with our government employing deft, principled diplomacy and steely military resolve to checkmate hardline PLA generals in Beijing.
   (III) Our Union Home Minister said that India has become a powerful nation and that is why it was able to resolve the standoff at Doklam with China. "Had India remained weak, the Doklam standoff would not have been resolved till now. It was possible only because India has become a world power," he said. Troops from India and China had been locked in a face off in the Doklam region for over two months. "Everyone was expecting that relation between China and India will deteriorate due to the Doklam issue, but both the countries resolved the issue with comprehension," he added.
   (a) Only (I) is correct   (b) Only (II) is correct
   (c) Only (III) is correct   (d) Both (I) and (III) are correct
   (e) All are correct

139. There is no provision for banning a film in the certification rule
   (I) Constitutional guarantees of freedom of expression are under threat in India. How can some people threaten to kill or maim persons associated with films they don't like and haven't even seen? Censorship is nothing but a dictatorial weapon used by people who do not want the public to know what is really happening in the country. Banning a movie is clearly not only illegal but shockingly naive and unwise.
   (II) Some of the burning issues that confront us are: How does the Constitution of India define freedom of speech and expression? What are the limits on the said freedom? Why are films banned? Are these bans constitutionally valid? What views have been expressed by the final interpreter of the Constitution, the Supreme Court of India, about these bans on the films? Are we on the right constitutional path when we ban films? What consequences would these bans have on our freedom of speech and expression and on the rule of law?

REVISION EXERCISES

(III) To ban a film in India, reacting to demands from some, is grave constitutional impropriety. We tolerate such foolish and sometimes dangerous appeals not because they may prove true but because freedom of speech is indivisible. That liberty cannot be denied to some ideas and saved for others. The endeavour here is to highlight that banning a film is not only unconstitutional and illegal but also imprudent.

(a) Only (I) is correct   (b) Only (II) is correct
(c) Only (III) is correct   (d) Both (I) and (III) are correct
(e) All are correct

140. Pollution is adversely affecting the health of children.

(I) A study conducted on Delhi children and released recently in the Journal of Indian Paediatrics provides powerful evidence that shows children growing up in polluted environments like the Capital have reduced lung growth compared to children in developed countries like the United States.

(II) Bad food habits is taking a toll on our children, warn doctors. A group of doctors have published a multi-centric study to drive home the ill effects of moving away from healthy eating habits and opting for easy-to-use and widely accessible processed food.

(III) Children living in big cities such as Delhi, are likely to grow susceptible to allergic ailments, more than adults, due to urban pollution, especially air, health experts said. Infants and children living in metro cities are inhaling polluted air and therefore their resistance to allergic ailments is lowered at a very young age, making them more susceptible to contract various allergies when they grow up, compared to adults.

(a) Only (I) is correct   (b) Only (II) is correct
(c) Only (III) is correct   (d) Both (I) and (III) are correct
(e) All are correct

SENTENCE FORMATION

DIRECTIONS (Qs. 141-150) : There are sets of four statements in question given below which when connected using the correct sentence structure forms a complete single sentence without altering the meaning of the sentences given in the question. There are four options given below the question, choose the sentence that forms the correct formation of single sentence which is both grammatically correct and contextually meaningful. If none follows, choose (e) as your answer.

141. It spent some percentage of its GDP on research and development; A chapter in the Economic Survey has data about India's spending on GDP; Last year, it spent only 0.5% of its GDP; It was far below its economic capacity on research.

(a) India spent far below its economical capacity on research last year, according to a chapter in the Economic Survey as its spending was only 0.5% of its GDP in research and development.

(b) As India spent only 0.5% of its GDP in research and development last year as per the data revealed by a page of the Economic Survey, it can be concluded that it spent far below its economical capacity on research.

(c) A page in the Economic Survey states that, India's expenditure on research and development was far below its economic capacity on research as it spent only 0.5% of its GDP on research and development.

(d) According to a chapter in the Economic Survey, India spent only 0.5% of its GDP on research and development in the last year which is far below its economic capacity on research.

(e) None of the above is correct

142. GST uses a unique modified deterrent behavioural model; It promotes tax compliance behaviour as a compulsion along with a self-promoting motive; But to shift from noncompliance to compliance we need a paradigm shift in culture; It is completely overlooked in any discussion on GST.

(a) To shift from non-compliance to compliance we need a paradigm shift in culture which is completely overlooked in any discussion on GST which uses a unique modified deterrent behavioural model that promotes tax compliance behaviour as a compulsion along with a self-promoting motive.

(b) GST uses a unique modified deterrent behavioural model, wherein it promotes tax compliance behaviour as a compulsion along with a self-profiting motive, however, to shift from non-compliance to compliance, we need a paradigm shift in culture, which is completely overlooked in any discussion on GST.

(c) To promote tax compliance behaviour GST uses a unique modified deterrent behavioural model which shifts from non-compliance to compliance as a paradigm shift in culture, is completely overlooked in any discussion on GST.

(d) A paradigm shift in culture of non-compliance to compliance is completely overlooked in any discussion on GST; that's why GST uses a unique modified deterrent behavioural model which promotes tax compliance behaviour.

(e) None of the above is correct

143. He invites as many technical people and academicians as he can for lunch; He spends an hour a day trawling the internet; He wants to act as a beacon for his version of the learning organization; He looks forward to learning about new technological developments in his field.

(a) In order to becoming a beacon for his version of the learning organization, he spent an hour a day trawling the internet so that he could find as many technical people and academicians as he can for lunch to learn about new technological developments in his field.

REVISION EXERCISES

(b) Since he wants to become a beacon for his version of the learning organization, he not only spends an hour a day trawling the internet to learn about new technological developments in his field but he too makes as many luncheon appointments as he can with technical people and academicians.

(c) To act as a beacon for his version of the learning organization, he not only spends an hour a day trawling the internet to learn about new technological developments in his field, he also makes as many luncheon appointments as he can with technical people and academicians.

(d) By inviting as many technical people and academicians as he can for lunch after trawling the internet for one hour every single day, he wishes to become a beacon for his version of the learning organization as he looks forward to learn about new technological developments in his field.

(e) All of the above are correct

144. Our law is not a monolith; It is not handed to us by our founding fathers as an edifice constructed brick-by-brick through an incremental series of decisions; It is not based on the judgements that preceded it; It is in aggregate a composite, well-integrated whole.

(a) Our law is not handed to us as a monolith constructed brick-by-brick through an incremental series of decisions based on the judgements preceding it but it is in aggregate a composite, well-integrated whole.

(b) Our law is well-integrated whole and not a monolith handed to us by our founding fathers constructed brick-by-brick through an incremental series of decisions based on the judgements that preceded it in aggregate.

(c) Our law is not a monolith handed to us by our founding fathers as an edifice constructed brick-by-brick through an incremental series of decision based on the judgements that preceded it but it is in aggregate a composite, well-integrated whole.

(d) The monolithic edifice constructed brick-by-brick by our forefathers, based on incremental series of decisions, is like our law which is in aggregate a composite, well-integrated whole.

(e) None of the above is correct

145. Fans are eagerly awaiting the finale of Season 7 of Game of Thrones; It will be aired on Monday in India; A south Delhi firm has begun work on the props and costumes; These props and costumes will be used in the next and final season of the popular television series.

(a) A South Delhi firm has began work on the props and costumes to be used in the next and final season of the popular television series which will be aired on Monday in India being waited eagerly by fans.

(b) The finale of Season 7 of Game of Thrones to be aired on Monday in India and props and costumes to be prepared by a South Delhi firm and to be used in the next and final season of the popular television series are being waited eagerly.

(c) The props and costumes to be used in the next and final season of the popular television series are being prepared by a South Delhi firm, which is being eagerly awaited by the fans to be aired on Monday in India.

(d) While fans are eagerly awaiting the finale of Season 7 of Game of Thrones, which will be aired on Monday in India, a South Delhi firm has begun work on the props and costumes to be used in the next and final season of the popular television series.

(e) None of the above is correct

146. It has continued with its underlying humour; Film 'Ant-Man was' successful; Marvel studios has made another movie whose lot of promotions were done earlier; Another superhero – The Wasp is added in the upcoming sequel which contains extra action.

(a) As the film 'Ant-Man' was successful, Marvel studios has come up with another movie whose lot of promotions were done earlier which introduces another superhero – The Wasp who will make sure that the underlying humour is maintained along with extra action.

(b) Another film with another superhero – The Wasp with extra humour and action has been made by Marvel studios which is a sequel to the successful movie 'Ant-Man'.

(c) Seeing the success of the film 'Ant-Man', Marvel studios has made another epic promotional sequel that contains new superhero- The Wasp, extra actions and underlying humour.

(d) Since the film 'Ant-Man' was successful, Marvel studios has made a sequel to it by adding another superhero – The Wasp, extra action and its underlying humour.

(e) None of the above is correct.

147. It was a hospital; The accident happened in West Delhi; Some patients were injured and suffered minor burns; On Sunday, a major fire broke out.

(a) In a accident of fire at a hospital in West Delhi on Sunday, some patients suffered minor burns and injuries.

(b) A major fire broke out on Sunday at a hospital in West Delhi in which some patients suffered injuries and minor burns.

(c) Some patients, in an accident on Sunday that occurred in a hospital in the Western part of Delhi suffered injuries and minor burns.

(d) Due to a fire broke out at a hospital in West Delhi on Sunday, some patients suffered injuries and minor burns.

(e) None of the above is correct

REVISION EXERCISES

148. She was weeping; They were returning home in a dark night; It was a late night party; They saw an old lady sitting on the road side.
    (a) A weeping old lady sitting on the road side in a dark night was seen by them who were returning back to home from a late night party.
    (b) As they were returning home in a dark night from a late night party, they saw an old lady which was sitting on the road side and weeping.
    (c) It was a dark night when they saw a weeping old lady sitting on the road side while they were on their way back home from a late night party.
    (d) An old weeping lady was seen by them who were on their way back to home from a late night party.
    (e) None of the above is correct
149. I hope to see him in the concert tonight; we were on the flight; I met him after eight years, he was sitting next to me; He will perform in the concert.
    (a) I met him after eight years on the flight as he was sitting next to me and I look forward to seeing him perform in the concert tonight.
    (b) I was on the flight after years where the person sitting next to me was him and I hope to see him perform in tonight's concert.
    (c) I met him after eight years on the flight, he is a performer and he would be performing in tonight's concert where I wish to see him.
    (d) After eight years, we met each other on the flight as we were fellow-passengers; moreover, I look forward to seeing him perform in the concert tonight.
    (e) None of the above is correct
150. England lost to India; Indian batsmen played extremely well; It was a duck soup for India; The total runs scored by them were only 102.
    (a) England outplayed India as they scored only 102 runs and Indian batsmen batted extremely well.
    (b) India managed to win the match against England as the target was only 102 and Indian batsmen batted extremely well.
    (c) It was an easy win against England as Indian batsmen played well enough to achieve the small target of 102.
    (d) India won the match against England easily because the total runs scored by them were only 102 and Indian batsmen batted superbly.
    (e) None of the above is correct

HINTS & SOLUTIONS

1.	(b)	26.	(c)	51.	(e)	76.	(b)	101.	(d)	126.	(a)
2.	(d)	27.	(d)	52.	(a)	77.	(d)	102.	(c)	127.	(c)
3.	(c)	28.	(e)	53.	(c)	78.	(e)	103.	(a)	128.	(e)
4.	(e)	29.	(c)	54.	(c)	79.	(a)	104.	(c)	129.	(b)
5	(a)	30.	(a)	55.	(c)	80.	(c)	105.	(e)	130.	(c)
6.	(b)	31.	(d)	56.	(d)	81.	(b)	106.	(d)	131.	(d)
7.	(d)	32.	(b)	57.	(b)	82.	(c)	107.	(e)	132.	(b)
8.	(d)	33.	(b)	58.	(c)	83.	(e)	108.	(b)	133.	(e)
9.	(c)	34.	(a)	59.	(e)	84.	(c)	109.	(a)	134.	(d)
10.	(b)	35.	(c)	60.	(a)	85.	(b)	110.	(d)	135.	(d)
11.	(d)	36.	(a)	61.	(c)	86.	(a)	111.	(a)	136.	(d)
12.	(b)	37.	(d)	62.	(b)	87.	(d)	112.	(e)	137.	(e)
13.	(c)	38.	(d)	63.	(d)	88.	(a)	113.	(a)	138.	(e)
14.	(a)	39.	(c)	64.	(e)	89.	(e)	114.	(c)	139.	(d)
15.	(e)	40.	(a)	65.	(c)	90.	(c)	115.	(c)	140.	(d)
16.	(a)	41.	(e)	66.	(a)	91.	(e)	116.	(c)	141.	(d)
17.	(c)	42.	(c)	67.	(d)	92.	(b)	117.	(b)	142.	(b)
18.	(e)	43.	(b)	68.	(c)	93.	(d)	118.	(e)	143.	(c)
19.	(b)	44.	(e)	69.	(c)	94.	(c)	119.	(b)	144.	(c)
20.	(d)	45.	(e)	70.	(d)	95.	(a)	120.	(c)	145.	(d)
21.	(b)	46.	(a)	71.	(b)	96.	(e)	121.	(b)	146.	(e)
22.	(e)	47.	(c)	72.	(e)	97.	(c)	122.	(b)	147.	(b)
23.	(a)	48.	(e)	73.	(d)	98.	(a)	123.	(b)	148.	(c)
24.	(d)	49.	(c)	74.	(e)	99.	(e)	124.	(c)	149.	(a)
25.	(c)	50.	(b)	75.	(a)	100.	(c)	125.	(a)	150.	(d)

www.ingramcontent.com/pod-product-compliance
Lightning Source LLC
LaVergne TN
LVHW021237080526
838199LV00088B/4558